Foreword

Dear student,

India. For many of us in the west the name conjures up exotic images of white palaces shimmering in the sun, women in saris, elephants and tigers …

But what is India really like? There are all kinds of reasons why you might be motivated to learn more about this complex and fascinating country, which despite its colonisation by Britain in the past has always managed to retain its own proud identity. Maybe you think it is essential to have some knowledge of the second most populous nation and largest democracy on earth because it is fast emerging as a new world power. Possibly you can imagine going there yourself at some point in the future and wish to understand the people and their traditions or you might want to explore the rich cultural heritage that has provided the world with influential philosophies and works of literature. On the other hand, perhaps your interest has been aroused by something as simple as wanting to know more about the land where your shirt was made, or watching a popular film set in India!

Whatever your starting point, one thing is sure: the more you discover about India, the more you will realise how much there is to explore. Hopefully this book will be the key to help you open the door to a whole new experience!

How to use this book and CD-ROM effectively

This book contains film and audio clips, internet links and a wide range of texts, from news articles to poems and literary extracts which will provide food for thought and encourage you to explore further.

The tasks are designed to give practical aid with analysis, while leaving room for creativity and providing exam practice for Abitur. With the vocab sheets on the CD-ROM you can build up your own range of words and expressions (see pages 58/59). The listening texts can be played either on a standard CD player or on the computer. In addition there are four group project suggestions for some task-based learning. You will find links to websites and online video clips at the top of the relevant pages. To view these online links, enter the number (for example [🖳 601006-0001]) in the search box on our homepage www.klett.de.

We hope this book will help you to develop as a speaker of English and participant in an intercultural dialogue that requires sensitive ears and minds.

Your **Abi Workshop** Team

Symbols and abbreviations

[👥]   Do this task with another person.
[👥👥]   Do this task in a (small) group.
[🎧]   This listening text is on the CD-ROM.
[🎬]   This film clip is on the CD-ROM.
[🖳]   You will need Internet access to complete this task.

adj	adjective	*e.g.*	*exempli gratia (Lat.)*	*obs*	obsolete, ouf of fashion
adv	adverb		= for example		
AE	American English	*esp*	especially	*sb*	somebody
↔	antonym	*fml*	formal	*sl*	slang
AUS	Australian English	*i.e.*	*id est (Lat.)* = that is	*sth*	something
BE	British English	*infml*	informal	*v*	verb
disappr	disapproving	*n*	noun, substantive		

Contents

Title	Text type	Source	
Topic 1 A plural country			
A plural country	Introduction		4
Indian identity is forged by diversity	Newspaper article	Shashi Tharoor, *The Guardian*	6
A visit to the Cow Product Research Centre	Book excerpt	From: Edward Luce, *In Spite of the Gods*	8
Listening/Mediation	Dialogue		9
Hindu Gods	Fact file on Hindu Gods		10
What Happened to the Elephant?	Poem	Sujata Bhatt	11
A visual dialect	Book excerpt	From: William Dalrymple, *The Age of Kali*	12
Topic 2 The wounds of history			
The wounds of history	History timeline		14
Why can't we be friends?	Novel excerpt	From: E.M. Forster, *A Passage to India*	15
Father to a nation, stranger to his son	Newspaper article	Sarfraz Manzoor, *The Guardian*	16
Cracking India	Novel excerpt	From: Bapsi Sidhwa, *Cracking India*	18
Spot on facts: Indian independence	Fact file on Indian independence		19
Exit wounds – The legacy of Indian Partition	Newspaper article	Pankaj Mishra, *The New Yorker*	20
Muslims – India's new 'untouchables'	Newspaper article	Asra Q. Nomani, *Los Angeles Times*	22
Looking across the border	Book excerpt	From Edward Luce, *In Spite of the Gods*	24
Indische Presse bezichtigt Pakistans Geheimdienst der Terrorhilfe	Internet news article	*Spiegel Online*	25
Topic 3 Different worlds			
Different worlds	Introduction		26
'Long live Suttee' cried the mob	Newspaper article	Luke Harding, *Asian News*	28
Hunger	Novel excerpt	From: Kamala Markandaya, *Nectar in a Sieve*	30
The Solitude of Emperors	Novel excerpt	From: David Davidar, *The Solitude of Emperors*	32
A shocking transformation	Interview transcript	From: *Channel 4 News*	34

Contents

Title	Text type	Source	
Topic 4 East meets West			
[🖥] India's magic works wonders!	Internet article	Vimla Patil, *South Asian Women's Forum*	36
A family of Anglophiles	Novel excerpt	From: Arundhati Roy, *The God of Small Things*	38
[📁] The world as India	Essay excerpt	From: Susan Sontag, "The World as India", in: *At the Same Time*	40
[◉] The Gateway of India [🖥]	Novella excerpt	From: Paul Theroux, "The Gateway of India", in: *The Elephanta Suite*	42
Fashion's dirty secret	Newspaper article	Dean Nelson, *The Sunday Times*	44
Träume in Pink, Gold, Orange	Newspaper article	Christiane Grefe, *Die Zeit*	45
[◉] Jasmine	Novel excerpt	From: Bharati Mukherjee, *Jasmine*	46
[◉] The Mistress of Spices	Novel excerpt	From: Chitra Banerjee Divakaruni, *The Mistress of Spices*	48

Projects		
[◉] **Project 1:**	A cultural trip to India	50
Project 2:	A literary contest	52
[🖥] **Project 3:**	Myths and legends	54
Project 4:	A taste of India	56

Worksheets		
Vocabulary work:	Text-based vocabulary files and thematic vocabulary files	58
Revision file 1:	A plural country (Topic 1)	60
Revision file 2:	The wounds of history (Topic 2)	61
Revision file 3:	Different worlds (Topic 3)	62
Revision file 4:	East meets West (Topic 4)	63

Topic 1   A plural country

Some quotes about India

»In India, I found a race of mortals living upon the earth, but not adhering to it, inhabiting cities, but not being fixed to them, possessing everything, but possessed by nothing.«

Apollonius Tyaneus (Greek traveller, 1st century)

»India was the motherland of our race, and Sanskrit the mother of Europe's languages: she was the mother of our philosophy; mother, through the Arabs, of much of our mathematics; mother, through the Buddha, of the ideals embodied in Christianity; mother, through the village community, of self-government and democracy. Mother India is in many ways the mother of us all.«

William James Durant (Philosopher and historian, 1885–1981)

1. What do you associate with India? Brainstorm for a list of key words. Write them down, leaving enough space to add more information to each of them while you work through this book.

2. a) Look at the woman in the yellow sari. Imagine who she might be, where and how she might have lived her life, what she might have felt on her skin when the picture was taken and why she believes that India is the best place in the world to be born right now.

   b) Explain which place would be the best place in the world to be born right now for you. Give reasons for your choice.

A plural country 1

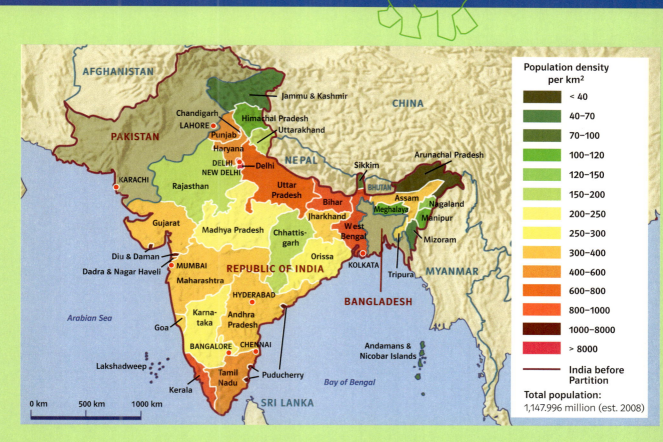

>> When I first visited, I was stunned by the richness of the land, by its lush beauty and exotic architecture, by its ability to overload the senses with the pure, concentrated intensity of its colours, smells, tastes, and sounds. It was as if all my life I had been seeing the world in black and white and, when brought face-to-face with India, experienced everything re-rendered in brilliant technicolor. <<

Keith Bellows (Vice president of the National Geographic Society, born 1953)

>> With one foot grounded in time-honored traditions and the other fervently striding into the entrepreneurial e-age, India embraces diversity passionately as few other countries on earth could. <<

Lonely Planet Guide (2001)

3 Examine and compare the three covers. Two of them were published in special editions to celebrate the 60th anniversary of India's independence, 15th August 2007. What picture of India do they convey? What aspects are dealt with? What symbols, motifs and language are used to bring about their messages?

4 Read the quotations by people who travelled India in different centuries.
   a) Summarise what each of them found the most fascinating aspect of the country and how they experienced it. Which aspect is most interesting to you?
   b) Compare what you have seen on these pages with the result of your brainstorming in exercise 1.

1 A plural country

1 *Collect ideas about what you think helps to create a feeling of national identity among the citizens of a country.*

Indian identity is forged in diversity

In this article, which appeared in a British newspaper, Indian diplomat and writer Dr. Shashi Tharoor considers the issue of Indian identity.

When India celebrated the 49th anniversary of its independence from British rule in 1996, its then prime minister, HD Deve Gowda, stood at the ramparts of Delhi's Red Fort and delivered the traditional independence day address to the nation. Eight other prime ministers had done exactly the same thing 48 times before him, but what was unusual this time was that Deve Gowda, a southerner from the state of Karnataka, spoke to the country in a language of which he did not know a word. Tradition and politics required a speech in Hindi, so he gave one – the words having been written out for him in his native Kannada script, in which they made no sense.

Such an episode is almost inconceivable elsewhere, but it was a startling affirmation of Indian pluralism. For the simple fact is that we are all minorities in India. There has never been an archetypal Indian to stand alongside the archetypal German or Frenchman. A Hindi-speaking Hindu male from Uttar Pradesh may cherish the illusion he represents the "majority community". But he does not. As a Hindu, he belongs to the faith adhered to by four-fifths of the population. But a majority of the country does not speak Hindi. And, if he were visiting, say, my home state of Kerala, he may be surprised to realise that a majority there is not even male.

Worse, this stock Hindu male has only to mingle with the polyglot, multicoloured crowds – and I am referring not to the colours of their clothes but to the colours of their skins – thronging any of India's major railway stations to realise how much of a minority he really is. Even his Hinduism is no guarantee of his majorityhood, because caste divisions automatically put him in a minority. (If he is a Brahmin, for instance, 90% of his fellow Indians are not.)

If caste and language complicate the notion of Indian identity, ethnicity makes it worse. Most of the time, an Indian's name immediately reveals where he is from or what her mother-tongue is: when we introduce ourselves, we are advertising our origins. Despite some intermarriage at the elite levels in our cities, Indians are still largely endogamous, and a Bengali is easily distinguishable from a Punjabi. The difference this reflects is often more apparent than the elements of commonality. A Karnataka Brahmin shares his Hindu faith with a Bihari Kurmi, but they share little identity with each other in respect of their dress, customs, appearance, taste, language or even, these days, their political objectives. At the same time, a Tamil Hindu would feel he has much more in common with a Tamil Christian or a Tamil Muslim than with, say, a Jat from the state of Haryana with whom he formally shares the Hindu religion.

What makes India, then, a nation? […]

Not language, since India's constitution now recognises 22 official languages, and as many as 35 languages spoken by more than a million people each. Not ethnicity, since the "Indian" accommodates a diversity of racial types in which many Indians (Punjabis and Bengalis, in particular) have more ethnically in common with foreigners than with their other compatriots. Not

TIP
Look at the map on the previous page to find the Indian states mentioned in the text. These adjectives/names for people from different regions are also in the text:
Bengal – Bengali
Punjab – Punjabi
Bihar – Bihari
Tamil Nadu – Tamil
Kerala – Keralite

FACT FILE
Over 1,600 languages and dialects are spoken in India. Apart from English, these are the twelve most important languages: Hindi, Bengali, Telugu, Marathi, Tamil, Urdu, Gujarati, Kannada, Malayalam, Oriya, Punjabi, Assamese.

[2] **HD Deve Gowda** born 1933, 12th prime minister of India 1996–97
[2] **rampart** defensive wall
[14] **to cherish** to keep (a hope) in one's mind
[19] **stock** *here:* typical
[21] **to throng** to fill (a place)
[23] **caste** [kɑːst] hereditary class of Hindu society
[24] **Brahmin** member of the highest caste
[30] **endogamous** marrying within one's community
[32] **commonality** the state of sharing characteristics
[33] **Kurmi** member of a low caste
[37] **Jat** member of a people in north-west India

A plural country

religion, since India is a secular pluralist state that is home to every religion known to mankind, with the possible exception of Shintoism. Not geography, since the natural geography of the subcontinent – framed by the mountains and sea – was hacked by the partition of 1947. And not even territory, since, by law, anyone with one grandparent born in pre-partition India - outside
50 the territorial boundaries of today's state – is eligible for citizenship. Indian nationalism has therefore always been the nationalism of an idea.

It is the idea of an ever-ever land – emerging from an ancient civilisation, united by a shared history, sustained by pluralist democracy. India's democracy imposes no narrow conformities on its citizens. The whole point of
55 Indian pluralism is you can be many things and one thing: you can be a good Muslim, a good Keralite and a good Indian all at once. The Indian idea is the opposite of what Freudians call "the narcissism of minor differences"; in India we celebrate the commonality of major differences. If America is a melting-pot, then to me India is a thali, a selection of sumptuous dishes in different
60 bowls. Each tastes different, and does not necessarily mix with the next, but they belong together on the same plate, and they complement each other in making the meal a satisfying repast.

So the idea of India is of one land embracing many. It is the idea that a nation may endure differences of caste, creed, colour, conviction, culture,
65 cuisine, costume and custom, and still rally around a consensus. And that consensus is around the simple idea that in a democracy you don't really need to agree – except on the ground rules of how you will disagree.

Geography helps, because it accustoms Indians to the idea of difference. India's national identity has long been built on the slogan "unity in diversity".
70 The "Indian" comes in such varieties that a woman who is fair-skinned, sari-wearing and Italian-speaking, as Sonia Gandhi is, is not more foreign to my grandmother in Kerala than one who is "wheatish-complexioned", wears a salwar kameez and speaks Urdu. Our nation absorbs both these types of people; both are equally "foreign" to some of us, equally Indian to us all.
75 For now, the sectarian Hindu chauvinists have lost the battle over India's identity. The sight in May 2004 of a Roman Catholic political leader (Sonia Gandhi) making way for a Sikh (Manmohan Singh) to be sworn in as prime minister by a Muslim (President Abdul Kalam) – in a country 81 % Hindu – caught the world's imagination. India's founding fathers wrote a constitution
80 for their dreams; we have given passports to their ideals. That one simple moment of political change put to rest many of the arguments over Indian identity. India was never truer to itself than when celebrating its own diversity.

Shashi Tharoor, *The Guardian*, August 15, 2007

⁴⁶**Shintoism** religion originating in Japan
⁴⁸**partition** division of India in 1947 to create Pakistan
⁵²**ever-ever land** a word created in analogy to never-never land, an imaginary dream world
⁵⁷**Freudian** supporter of Sigmund Freud's psychological theories
⁵⁷**narcissism** looking at and being in love with oneself
⁵⁹**sumptuous** luxurious
⁶²**repast** *(fml)* meal
⁶⁵**to rally around** to come together to support
⁷⁰**sari** length of silk or cotton wrapped around the body
⁷¹**Sonia Gandhi** Italian-born (1946) Indian politician, widow of assassinated prime minister Rajiv Gandhi
⁷³**salwar kameez** loose-fitting trousers and tunic

WORD BANK
The way people see themselves … • From the outside … • clichés and stereotypes • … is typically associated with … • Identity can be based on … • What you feel for your home depends on … • be part of a community • … contributes to a feeling of togetherness • keep up traditions • … makes a place and its people unique

2 a) *Develop a mind map around the concept of 'Indian diversity'.*
b) *Evaluate if your ideas for ex. 1 are suitable to describe Indian identity.*

3 a) *Scan the text for references to the principles of government in India.*
b) *Examine the concept of the Indian nation presented in the text. Point out what stylistic devices the author uses to support his view. Then comment on his attitude.*

4 [👥] *Write a text outlining your ideas about German identity at the beginning of the 21st century. Then swap texts with a partner, read each other's texts and comment on their language and content.*

1 A plural country

Venkateswara Temple, Tirumala

Darbar Sahib (Golden Temple), Amritsar

Jama Masjid Mosque, Delhi

A visit to the Cow Product Research Centre

Although India is a secular state, there is a strong Hindu nationalist movement that seeks to promote the influence of Hinduism in all aspects of life, including the role of the sacred cow. The following text is an extract from a book about modern India by British author Edward Luce.

I decided to visit the Cow Product Research Centre near Nagpur. Run by the VHP, the centre seeks to build on the five traditional village products of the cow: milk, ghee (clarified butter), butter, urine (for religious purposes) and dung (for fuel). I was accompanied by Sunil Mansinghka, a senior VHP activist. The centre, which draws on the research skills of dozens of young men with Ph.D.s in medicine and biology, also runs a hostel and a school for the local tribal population that is named after Swami Vivekananda, a widely respected Hindu philosopher and social reformer. "Please remove your *chappals* [sandals]," said Mansinghka as we approached a vast cow shed. "What, barefoot?" I asked, with an eye on the puddles of cow urine and cow dung that covered the ground. "Yes, barefoot," he replied. "Cow dung is an antiseptic. If you have athlete's foot, you will be cured."

Outside the cow shelter there was a notice which said: "Do not tease the cow, give it love. Spitting is prohibited inside. Give any donations and offerings to the worker not to the cow." I stepped gingerly into the shelter, trying not to slip. Mansinghka said: "These cows are the pure cow breeds of Hindustan. We have spent a long time separating the foreign cow breeds from the indigenous breeds, which are much superior in every way." He wheeled me face to face with a very fierce-looking bull, whose vast dangling testicles were the size of cricket balls. I recoiled. "Do not worry," said Mansinghka, wheeling me back to face the bull, "it is a pure Indian breed. It cannot hurt you. Not like the bulls in the west." I was pushed eyeball to eyeball with the bull for a snap second. Then I was somehow manoeuvred through the two-inch layer of cow product to the middle of the herd. I was handed a silver tray with candles on it and also turmeric, rice, flowers and red paste. I had to circle the tray a few times above the head of one of the cows before smearing the paste on the cow's forehead and my own. "Now you are praying to the cow. She is my mother. She is your mother," said Mansinghka. Mother seemed unfazed by all the attention.

Then I was taken to the laboratories. The first room hit me about twenty metres before we arrived. It contained hundreds of bottles of cow's urine,

---

FACT FILE

Religion in India
Approximately 80.5% of the Indian population are **Hindus**. Roughly 13.4% of the population are **Muslims**.

The three other native religions are **Jainism**, **Buddhism** and **Sikhism**, which together account for about 3.8%.

About 2.3% of people in India are **Christians**. A few thousand **Jews** also live there, as do the same number of **Zoroastrians** (named after their prophet, Zarathustra, and called **Parsees** in India because of their Persian origin).

---

[1] **Nagpur** city in the state of Maharashtra
[4] **VHP** = Vishwa Hindu Parishad, World Council of Hinduism
[6] **Ph.D.** = Doctor of Philosophy
[12] **athlete's foot** infection of the skin between the toes
[15] **gingerly** carefully
[16] **Hindustan** historical name for Indian subcontinent
[19] **to dangle** to hang down
[19] **testicles** *Hoden*
[20] **to recoil** to jump back in fear
[25] **turmeric** a yellow Indian spice *(Kurkuma)*
[28] **unfazed** unimpressed, not concerned

A plural country

stacked up, one upon the other. There were Bunsen burners and some of the urine was bubbling away in beakers. "This is an antioxidant that will cure cancer," said one of the lab researchers, waving a capsule under my nose. Then there were urine-derivative products which cured bronchitis and obesity, one
35 which gave energy, and another that purified blood. Next we were shown cow dung products. Cow dung, too, conceals an impressive range of world-beating cures. My favourite product was cow-dung soap. There was also a cow-dung shampoo for dandruff. Mansinghka said the centre had submitted a number of cow-derivative applications to the US Patents Office and other countries.
40 "God lives in the cow dung," he said. "All of these recipes are contained in the holy texts."

   Mr Mansinghka, a Rajasthani in his late thirties, told me that there was no medicine outside of the Vedas that was worth using. It occurred to me that he was utterly sincere. Taken together, his beliefs amounted to textbook
45 fundamentalism – a modern condition in which you take the beliefs that people in the past had on some level accepted as symbolic and hold them to be literally true, and even scientifically demonstrable: God made the world in six days; Eve was formed from Adam's rib; Ram was born on this precise spot; and so on. But the Cow Research Centre did have some impressive uses
50 for cow's product. Mansinghka showed me several trees, each of which had been fertilised with specially enriched cow biomass. Every leaf emitted a concentrated odour of the fruit of the tree – be it mangoes, lemons or oranges. This seemed very pleasant. And for all the science I know perhaps cow's urine really can cure cancer.
55   At the end of the tour Mansinghka, who had been looking throughout for some sign that I had been converted to the merits of the holy cow's products, said: "When you write, please be kind to the cow. She is our mother." I was happy to promise not to disrespect cows. When we had returned to Nagpur and were dropping Mansinghka off at the VHP offices, on the street just
60 outside the entrance there was a cow with its head stuck in a large pile of rubbish, chewing through plastic. It was an everyday scene, even in Nagpur, the capital of the cow protection movement. Nobody seemed to mind.

From: Edward Luce, *In Spite of the Gods*, 2006

[32] **beaker** glass container
[34] **obesity** state of being too fat
[36] **to conceal** to hide
[38] **dandruff** small pieces of dead skin among one's hair
[43] **Vedas** ancient Indian scriptures of knowledge
[48] **Ram** incarnation of Hindu god Vishnu

1 On the basis of the text above, say how you would respond to an invitation to visit the Cow Product Research Centre, and why.

2 Analyse the writer's attitude to what he experienced and the means by which he conveys this to the reader.

3 a) [👥] Using the impression you get of the writer's behaviour during his visit as a starting point, discuss what is or is not the appropriate way to react to unfamiliar customs or ways of thinking while in a foreign country.

   b) Discuss what topics of conversation can be 'dangerous' in intercultural exchanges and why.

4 [🔊] **Listening/Mediation:** You are with a group of German tourists in Delhi and have returned to your hotel after a visit to the Hindu Akshardham temple complex. One of your party, who speaks very little English, cannot understand what is being said by an Indian hotel guest trying to talk to her, and would like you to help. Listen, and whenever you hear the buzzer, act as interpreter. Your task is to achieve successful communication and a smooth intercultural exchange.

> **WORD BANK**
> **Talking about how to react to other cultures**
> (in)appropriate • to show respect • to cause offence • preconceived ideas • to open/close one's mind to • (dis)respectful • to have consideration for

> **WORD BANK**
> May I ...? • My friend is very concerned that ... • Thank you for being so understanding. • Do you mind if I ask ...? • Thank you so much.

1 A plural country

[🖥 Online-Link: 601006-0004]

Hindu gods

FACT FILE

Lakshmi

Although Hindus have a multiplicity of gods they may worship, these deities do not have a completely independent existence from one another. Instead, they are all manifestations of one or more of the many aspects of the Supreme Being. Hindus might pray to Lakshmi, for example, if they wish for either material or spiritual wealth. On the other hand, if their goal is to achieve knowledge, they can worship Saraswati.

Fundamental to the Hindu religion is the concept of reincarnation, a constant and everlasting cycle of repeated births and deaths. Like everything else, this cosmic cycle is guided and controlled by the one Supreme Being, whose activities in this context are represented by a trinity of deities. Brahma is the creator of life, Vishnu preserves and maintains the universe, and Shiva is associated with the principles of death and recreation.

For Hindus, religion is very much a part of daily life and they surround themselves with images of their gods, not only in grand and ornate temples, but also in their homes. The form in which deities are shown usually symbolises their particular powers. There are also gods that reflect the natural world in India, like the monkey-god Hanuman, or Ganesha, whose father Shiva cut off his head in anger and then replaced it with the head of an elephant.

WORD BANK

patron goddess • to be named after • cycle of death and rebirth • holy • divine • to immerse in water • to cleanse • to wash away sins • to cure ills • devout • to bless • to come from/return to the elements

1 a) [🎬] *First watch the video without writing anything down. Concentrate on what you see and then describe the scenes or images that remain most clearly in your mind.*

b) *Watch again, this time taking notes. Then answer the following questions on the main themes dealt with in the video:*
  1. Kali: *Why is this goddess important in Kolkata? What aspect of Hinduism is she especially associated with?*
  2. The Ganges: *What powers do Hindus ascribe to the river and what role does it play in their lives? What are the "contradictions" the commentator talks about in this context?*
  3. Kali Puja: *What time of day does this ceremony take place and what happens during it? In what way can it be compared with Christianity?*

WORD BANK

an innocent view of the world • the harsh realities of life • to be reflected in • a chain of questions • one life linked to another • circular movement • the use of repetition • to run on from one line to another • to mirror the movement

2 a) *Read the poem on the opposite page. Identify where and how the viewpoint changes. Sum up the contrast in the focus of the lyrical 'I' in the two parts of the poem.*

b) *Talk about the ways in which both the structure and the content of the poem reflect the Hindu concept of the cosmic cycle.*

c) *Examine the poetic devices used in the poem. Pick out words and phrases that help to create a contrast in mood and tone between the first and second halves. Find examples of sounds, rhythm or sentence structure that emphasise the content being expressed.*

d) *Discuss your interpretation of the last three lines.*

3 [👥] *Do your own research on one of the following themes and give a presentation in class.*
  - *popular Hindu festivals: their significance and how they are celebrated*
  - *The Ramayana: a synopsis of the story*
  - *one of the other religions native to India: Sikhism, Buddhism or Jainism*

A plural country

What Happened to the Elephant?

What happened to the elephant,
the one whose head Shiva stole
to bring his son Ganesh back to life?

This is the child's curiosity
the nosy imagination that continues
probing, looking for a way
to believe the fantasy
a way to prolong the story.

If Ganesh could still be Ganesh
with an elephant's head,
then couldn't the body of that elephant
find another life
with a horse's head – for example?

And if we found
a horse's head to revive
the elephant's body –
Who is the true elephant?
And what shall we do
about the horse's body?

Still, the child refuses
to accept Shiva's carelessness
and searches for a solution
without death

But now when I gaze
at the framed postcard
of Ganesh on my wall,
I also picture a rotting carcass
of a beheaded elephant
lying crumpled up
on its side, covered with bird shit
vulture shit –

Oh that elephant
whose head survived
for Ganesh –

He died, of course, but the others
in his herd, the hundreds
in his family must have found him.
They stared at him for hours
with their slow swaying sadness …
How they turned and turned
in a circle, with their trunks
facing outwards and then inwards
towards the headless one.

That is a dance
a group dance
no one talks about.

Sujata Bhatt

⁵**nosy** curious • ⁶**to probe** to investigate • ⁸**to prolong** to make longer • ¹⁵**to revive** to restore to life • ²⁵**framed** *eingerahmt* • ²⁷**carcass** dead body of an animal • ²⁸**to behead** to cut sb's head off • ²⁹**crumpled up** *here:* bent and collapsed • ³¹**vulture** *Geier* • ³⁹**to sway** to move slowly from side to side • ⁴¹**trunk** the long nose of an elephant

Ganesha

Shiva

VIP FILE

Sujata Bhatt was born in Ahmedabad, India in 1956 and grew up in India and the United States. She has won many awards for her poetry, which often shows a preoccupation with the theme of cultural identity. She now lives and works in Germany.

1 A plural country

FACT FILE
Rajasthan is the largest state in the Republic of India. It is situated in the northwest and has a very old and rich history. It includes the greater part of the Thar Desert and the Aravalli Range, one of the oldest mountain ranges in the world. Rajasthan is famous for its rich cultural heritage, and a lot of ancient palaces, forts and temples can be seen there.

¹**to scorch** to burn
¹**scrub** land with few plants
²**dust-devil** small whirlwind
²**to grit** to spread sand over sth
⁴**octogenarian** an 80 to 89-year-old person
⁷**to encroach** to enter a place belonging to sb else
⁹**muttonchop whiskers** *Backenbart*
¹⁴**Jodhpur** city in Rajasthan
¹⁶**ridge** top of a mountain range
¹⁷**bluff** cliff
¹⁹**thatched** made of straw
²³**pukka** *(Hindi)* superior
²⁴**Harijan** lowest caste, known as Untouchables
³²**charpoy** *(Urdu)* daybed
⁴²**saffron** *(colour)* Safran
⁴³**dhoti** *(Hindi)* cloth worn by men around the hips

A visual dialect

British travel writer William Dalrymple describes what he learns from Dr Tyagi, who runs a medical centre for lower castes in the part of Rajasthan he is visiting.

The countryside was scorched white desert: hot, flat scrub, all sand-flats and dust-devils. As we drove through it the light sand rose in clouds, gritting my mouth and powdering my hair, so that I emerged from the car like some stage octogenarian. A hundred years ago there was jungle here, but the tree-fellers came and now there is only the occasional flowering shrub, the odd cactus or thicket of desert thorn.

Yet there are still villages here, fighting back the encroaching dunes, and when you see their people – women carrying water, yellow saris billowing in the desert wind, and tribesmen with muttonchop whiskers and mountainous turbans – it seems to the foreign eye as if they are growing almost organically out of the dust, and that what you are seeing is something good, and natural, and harmonious.

But the foreign eye is easily misled, and it cannot read the visual language of the villages. Driving back to Jodhpur from Dr Tyagi's field centre the following morning, I was shown just how deeply caste is written in to the Indian landscape. Coming over a ridge we saw ahead of us, perched on top of a slight bluff, a small white-stone village. To its side, a short distance away, stood another, larger, settlement: a series of round mud huts with pretty conical thatched roofs. Between the two, a chain of camels lurched along, moving in that strangely beautiful, seasick motion that camels break in to on sand dunes. To me it was a charming picture; but to Dr Tyagi it spoke of repression and caste-apartheid.

"The stone village with the *pukka* houses belongs to Rajputs. The huts belong to the *Harijans*. They are not allowed to live together, and if a *Harijan* wishes to come past the Rajput houses he must remove his shoes."

"Do the castes have separate wells?"

"No, there is only one well. If a woman from a Harijan family wishes to take water from the public well, a person of high caste must come and provide it. The Untouchable cannot touch the bucket. It is the same in every sphere of life. In the village tea-house, the cups for the *Harijans* are kept separately and at a distance from the cups of the other castes. If there is a public meeting, the *Harijans* cannot share the same *durree* [carpet] or *charpoy* as the Rajputs. If *Harijan* children are admitted to the primary school, then they must sit on the floor."

In Rajasthan, explained Dr Tyagi, caste was an open book which could be read as soon as you knew the local visual dialect. Once learnt, it enabled the onlooker to place, exactly, any individual in the rigid social hierarchy which for centuries has ranked and divided the villagers of India. The language changed from district to district, but among men it was usually the colour and tying of the turban that was significant: around Jodhpur, a white turban belonged to an elderly smallholder of the middle castes – the Bishnoi or the Jats – while a high-caste Brahmin would wear only saffron. The way you trained your moustache – upwards, downwards, or across – and the knot with which you tied your *dhoti* defined you even more closely, and could show even your sub-caste.

Among women it was jewellery and dress colour that was important: blue was the colour of the upper castes, and was worn with heavy ear- and nose-rings. In Jodhpur, the Brahmins even painted their houses blue. Red and green

A plural country

checks, yellow and mustard were worn by the middle castes, while darker colours, coarse cloth and simple silver anklets defined their wearer as low caste – or an outcaste, an Untouchable.

In the West, as everywhere in the world, there is a caste system of sorts, and dress is an important element of it: a pinstripe suit and tie places the wearer in one caste, a workman's dirty overalls in another. What is different about the Indian model is its rigidity and its central place in Hindu philosophy.

In much of rural India, caste still defines not only what you wear, but where you live, what trade you follow, whom you marry, even the colour you paint your home. Every detail of life in the traditional Indian village, where 80 per cent of Indians still live, is regulated. But if this is restrictive – and at its worst it is a form of divinely ordained serfdom – it can also be reassuring, a protection against anarchy. Beneath India's apparent chaos lies a rigid network of three thousand minutely graduated castes and sub-castes. Everyone knows his place, and exactly what is expected of him. Orthodox Hindus believe that your caste in this life is determined by your actions in a previous one. A good life is rewarded by high caste, a bad life punished by untouchability. A good roadsweeper can hope to be reincarnated next time round as a Brahmin, and thence eventually to achieve *moksha* or *nirvana*, so escaping the eternal cycle of suffering and rebirth.

Therefore, in the eyes of pious and traditional Hindus, to rise out of your caste does more than just rock the foundations of society: it breaks the cosmic cycle, it defies nature. So when a man tries to educate the *Dalits*, he must be stopped. And when a government commits itself to raising the status of the lower castes, to reserving government jobs for India's 152 million Untouchables, that too must be fought. As the Prime Minister V.P. Singh discovered to his cost in October 1990, the upper castes have no option: they must stand together and declare caste war.

From: William Dalrymple, *The Age Of Kali*, 1998

⁴⁸ **mustard** *(colour) Senf*
⁴⁹ **anklet** *Fußkettchen*
⁵² **pinstripe** cloth with a very narrow stripe
⁵⁹ **divine** related to the gods
⁵⁹ **to ordain** to determine
⁵⁹ **serfdom** slavery
⁶⁶ **moksha** *(in Hinduism and Jainism)* freedom from cycle of rebirth
⁶⁶ **nirvana** *(in Buddhism)* transcendent state of perfect happiness
⁶⁸ **pious** very religious
⁷⁰ **Dalit** member of the lowest caste
⁷³ **V.P. Singh** (1931–2008) Indian Prime Minister who was forced to resign in 1990 after his attempt to create a more equal society by reserving almost half of government jobs for the lower castes was met by protests and violence

1 a) *Compare and contrast what Dalrymple sees with what Dr Tyagi sees.*
b) *Collect examples from the text to explain what is meant by a 'visual dialect'. What is the author's intention in presenting it?*

2 *Explain the stabilising effect of the caste system on society that is mentioned in the text, and discuss your views on this.*

3 *Comment on the idea that there is 'a caste system of sorts' in the West.*

Brahmins
Kshatriyas
Vaishyas
Shudras
Untouchables

FACT FILE

The history of the caste system in India
The original Hindu system of caste (from the Portuguese word 'casta', meaning 'race') was based on ancient religious texts. It defined four castes according to their spiritual and physical development and self-control and did not explicitly exclude movement from one caste to another. Later the four castes were linked inseparably to the function individuals had in society. The highest caste, the **Brahmins**, were the intellectual and spiritual guides, priests and philosophers. Second were the **Kshatriyas**, the caste of warriors and rulers. Then came the **Vaishyas**, associated with trading and commerce, and the lowest caste were the **Shudras**, labourers and craftsmen. For fear of pollution, higher castes had to avoid any contact with the **'untouchables'**, people who ranked below all others and did the dirty work. Since 1949 the Constitution of India has granted all its citizens equal rights, but social change has been slow. The changes brought about by the **Industrial Revolution** and today's **economic boom** have done much more to weaken the caste system, and especially in the big cities it is losing influence. Where so many people are crowded together, pollution laws can no longer be observed, and it has also become possible to improve status through professional and financial success. The majority of the former untouchables, who now call themselves **Dalits** (the oppressed), are still underprivileged, but as their numbers are strong (18–20% of the population), democracy has equipped them with more power to fight for their rights.

Topic 2 The wounds of history

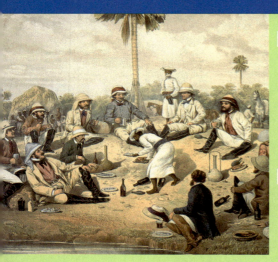

16th/17th century — Europeans start trading in India.

1600 — British **East India Trading Company** founded.

1757 — Beginning of **Company rule** in India.

1784 — Indian Act: British Parliament sets up a control board to restrict the Company's power.

19th century — **Expansion** of Company territories. British Parliament opens up the subcontinent to private investment and missionaries. **Positive developments**: During the Industrial Revolution an efficient infrastructure is set up. **Negative**: Market risks are shifted to the Indian taxpayers, skilled jobs are reserved for Europeans. The British Empire is flourishing: Britain imports raw materials from the colonies and exports manufactured goods to them. India is the 'Jewel in the Crown of the British Empire'.

1857 — **Indian Rebellion**: Indians resent land taxation by the British and interference with traditional inheritance laws. They also fear the British might try to impose Christianity on them and force them to abandon their traditional way of life. This leads to outbreaks of violence, brutally ended by the British.

1858 — Government of India Act: **Beginning of the British Raj**. The East India Company is dissolved. The Crown takes over rule with a Secretary of State for India and a Council of India in London. In Calcutta, the Viceroy is head of the central government of British India. The subordinate provinces each have their own governor. India consists of British India and over 600 native states governed by Indian princes. Power over the larger native states is held by the central government, the remaining states are under provincial government.

1876 — Queen Victoria becomes **Empress of India**.

Late 19th century — First steps towards self-government: Indian counsellors.

1885 — **Indian National Congress** is formed.

1892 — Indian Councils Act: Local administration included elected Indian members.

1906 — **All India Muslim League** is founded.

1909 — Government of India Act: Indian participation in legislative councils.

1914–1919 — **World War I**: India provides money and troops for the war.

1935 — Government of India Act: Independent legislative assemblies, central government for all the states, protection of Muslim minorities.

1937 — Nationwide **elections** for provincial assemblies, dominated by the Congress.

1939 — Beginning of **World War II**: The Viceroy declares war without the consent of Indian leaders. The Congress protests, Muslim leaders support Britain's war efforts.

1940 — Lahore/Pakistan Resolution: The Muslim League supports the idea of a separate **Muslim territory**. The Congress strongly objects. Violence between Hindus and Muslims ensues.

1942 — Mahatma Gandhi starts his 'Quit India' movement. Escalation of violence.

August 15, 1947 — British withdrawal. India becomes **independent**, but is **partitioned** into two separate states: India and Pakistan.

---

1 [2 ◉] *Listen to the first track and take notes to answer the following questions:*
   a) *What information does Mark Tully, a radio journalist for the BBC in India for over twenty years and thus an expert on India, give about the events in 1947 and how his family experienced them?*
   b) *What does 'going jungly' mean and what did most British people think of it?*

2 [3 ◉] *Listen to the second track and take notes. In what way is the second track related to the first one? Consider time, place, communicative situation and content.*

The wounds of history 2

Why can't we be friends?

The novel A Passage to India, *which is set in India during the British Raj, and deals with the British-Indian relationship, ends with this exchange between Dr Aziz, a Muslim physician, and Cyril Fielding, a British headmaster.*

Aziz grew more excited. He rose in his stirrups and pulled at his horse's head in the hope that it would rear. Then he should feel in a battle. He cried: "Clear out, all you Turtons and Burtons. We wanted to know you ten years back – now it's too late. If we see you and sit on your committees, it's for political reasons, don't you
5 make any mistake." His horse did rear. "Clear out, clear out, I say. Why are we put to so much suffering? We used to blame you, now we blame ourselves, we grow wiser. Until England is in difficulties we keep silent, but in the next European war – aha, aha! Then is our time." He paused, and the scenery, though it smiled, fell like a gravestone on any human hope. […]
10 "Who do you want instead of the English? The Japanese?" jeered Fielding, drawing rein.
"No, the Afghans. My own ancestors."
"Oh, your Hindu friends will like that, won't they?"
"It will be arranged – a conference of oriental statesmen." […]
15 Still he couldn't quite fit in Afghans at Mau, and, finding he was in a corner, made his horse rear again until he remembered that he had, or ought to have, a mother-land. Then he shouted: "India shall be a nation! No foreigners of any sort! Hindu and Moslem and Sikh and all shall be one! Hurrah! Hurrah for India! Hurrah! Hurrah!"
20 India a nation! What an apotheosis! Last comer to the drab nineteenth-century sisterhood! Waddling in at this hour of the world to take her seat! She, whose only peer was the Holy Roman Empire, she shall rank with Guatemala and Belgium perhaps! Fielding mocked again. And Aziz in an awful rage danced this way and that, not knowing what to do, and cried: "Down with the English
25 anyhow. That's certain. Clear out, you fellows, double quick, I say. We may hate one another, but we hate you most. If I don't make you go, Ahmed will, Karim will, if it's fifty or five hundred years we shall get rid of you, yes, we shall drive every blasted Englishman into the sea, and then" – he rode against him furiously – "and then," he concluded, half kissing him, "you and I shall be friends."
30 "Why can't we be friends now?" said the other, holding him affectionately. "It's what I want. It's what you want."
But the horses didn't want it – they swerved apart; the earth didn't want it, sending up rocks through which riders must pass single-file; the temples, the tank, the jail, the palace, the birds, the carrion, the Guest House, that came into
35 view as they issued from the gap and saw Mau beneath: they didn't want it, they said in their hundred voices, "No, not yet," and the sky said, "No, not there."

From: E. M. Forster, *A Passage to India*, 1924

VIP FILE

E.M. Forster (1879–1970); English writer; his work displays sharp, amusing observation of Victorian values and social conventions. His most famous novels are *A Room with a View* (1907) and *A Passage to India* (1924).

[1] **stirrup** *Steigbügel*
[2] **to rear** to rise on its hind legs
[11] **rein** *Zügel*
[20] **apotheosis** highest point of sth
[20] **drab** grey, dull
[21] **to waddle** *watscheln*
[22] **peer** person of equal rank
[32] **to swerve** to take a sudden turn
[33] **single-file** one behind the other
[34] **carrion** decaying flesh of dead animals

1 Describe and analyse the relationship between Aziz and Fielding as revealed by their behaviour and feelings.

2 Examine important aspects of the text (genre, narrator, point of view, characters, plot, theme, imagery, symbolism, structure etc.) in detail and use your results to illustrate how Forster portrays the situation in India at the time and the relationship between the Indians and the British in general.

2 The wounds of history

Father to a nation, stranger to his son

Mahatma Gandhi once confessed that the greatest regret of his life was that there were two people he had not been able to convince. One was Mohammed Ali Jinnah, whose demand for a separate homeland for Muslims led to the partition of India and Pakistan in August 1947 and the end of the dream of a united, independent India. The other person was his own eldest son. Harilal Gandhi's entire life was lived in the shadow of his father and it was spent rebelling against everything his father believed in. Gandhi's stern morality, sexual abstinence and principled stand against Britain were all challenged by his son, who was an alcoholic gambler trading in imported British clothes even as his father was urging a boycott of foreign goods. Harilal even converted to Islam and changed his name to Abdullah before his death in 1948, only months after his father was assassinated by a Hindu extremist.

Sixty years on from the Indian independence he was so instrumental in securing, Gandhi is a symbol of innocence and peace; a simple man in peasant clothes whose adherence to nonviolence defeated the British and would later inspire both Martin Luther King and Nelson Mandela. This was the Gandhi depicted in Richard Attenborough's multi-Oscar-winning film a quarter of a century ago: a dhoti-clad demigod. Attenborough's film told the story of Gandhi as the father of a nation; now a new film, *Gandhi, My Father*, reveals the extraordinary story of the son and the man he described as "the greatest father you can have but the one father I wish I did not have". The film's release coincides with the publication of a monumental new biography by Rajmohan Gandhi, a historian and grandson of the Mahatma. "I wrote this book because I wanted to make sense of my grandfather," says Rajmohan, 72. "I was 12 years old when my grandfather died and I wanted to be able to tell my children and grandchildren who Gandhi really was. The story of Gandhi is not only the story of India and partition: it is also the story of a father with high expectations and four sons who found it hard to measure up." […]

Gandhi's political philosophy was based on the belief that there was a larger good for society which demanded that each individual makes sacrifices. The necessity not to appear hypocritical meant that his sons were schooled at home when the family lived in South Africa. He could not have sent the boys to the private European schools without alienating himself from the Indian community, but in remaining true to his principles, he angered his children, who would meet other youngsters demanding to know which school they attended. […]

When an Indian friend offered Gandhi the opportunity to send one of his sons to England on a scholarship, Gandhi inquired whether the scholarship was truly for one of his boys or for the most deserving young person from the Indian community in South Africa. The man reluctantly agreed that the scholarship could go to the most deserving young person. Gandhi promptly suggested two other boys who he believed were more deserving and these were sent to England in the place of his own children. "You want to make saints out of my boys before they are men," complained his wife but, for Gandhi, his sons were to be the ideal symbols of the new India he was trying to create.

Embittered, Harilal resolved to carve out his own identity. He began drinking and trading in foreign clothes for profit; Gandhi's relationship with his son was further strained by Harilal's decision to remarry after the

---

VIP FILE

Mohandas Karamchand Gandhi, mostly called 'Mahatma' (Great Soul).
- born in 1869 in Gujarat, assassinated in 1948
- studied law in London
- stayed in South Africa 1893–1915 to represent Indian labourers, where he developed his famous philosophy of satyagraha, "a force born of truth combined with love"
- applied nationwide satyagraha actions of non-violent resistance in the Indians' struggle for independence from Britain
- sought to improve the conditions of the members of the lowest castes

---

²**Mohammed Ali Jinnah** (1876–1948) Indian statesman and first Governor General and President of Pakistan
⁷**stern** strict
⁹**gambler** Spieler
¹⁴**peasant** farm labourer
¹⁵**adherence to** strong and lasting support of (an idea)
¹⁷**Richard Attenborough** British film director
²¹**release** *here:* making a film available for viewing
²²**to coincide with** to occur at the same time as
²⁸**to measure up** to meet expectations
³¹**hypocritical** claiming falsely to be a good person
³⁸**scholarship** payment given for a student's education
⁴⁹**to strain** *here:* to put under tension

death of his first wife. "How can I who has always advocated renunciation of sex encourage you to gratify it?" asked Gandhi. "If Harilal wants to marry against my wish, I will have to stop thinking of him as my son." While Gandhi espoused nonviolence, his son's business at one point depended on the continuation of the second world war, and peace led to financial troubles. […]

Gandhi, My Father opens with Harilal's death after he is picked up from the streets in Mumbai and taken to hospital. The doctors imagine him to be an alcoholic vagrant. They ask him his father's name and he replies: "Bapu" – the term of endearment that Indians used to refer to Gandhi. The doctors agree that Bapu is indeed the father of the nation but demand the name of his biological father. It is a poignant scene. "Gandhi is an inconvenient truth," admits [director Feroz Abbas] Khan, "and his principles were hard to live by."

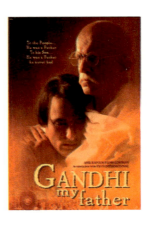

Filmed in English and Hindi and shot in India and South Africa, *Gandhi, My Father* is not typical Bollywood fare. Rather than the usual Bombay mix of melodrama and music, first-time director Khan's film is understated and humane. Khan based his script on his own play, *Mahatma vs Gandhi*; he supplemented the work with research visits to South Africa and interviews with Gandhi's relatives, all the while collecting letters, articles and any other scraps of information that would help make his film appear authentic.

"I have a responsibility to this subject and the dignity of the subject," he says. "There are no duets sung between Harilal and his father because they didn't have duets – they had arguments." Those arguments stemmed from Gandhi's belief that the needs of the nation were more important than the need of any individual. "One reason that Indians loved him so much," explains Rajmohan, "was that he was not partial to his children – that was his strongest card. He knew that if India wanted to be inspired, they needed the sort of leader who was willing to 'neglect' his children."

In fact, he was a fragile, troubled father. "People assume he was a miracle worker from the start," says Rajmohan, "some impossibly wonderful human being always in control of himself. This was not the case at all." Even before the film's release in India there were protests from those uncomfortable with this portrayal and demands that the film be banned.

Razi Ahmad, secretary of Gandhi Sangrahalaya, a research centre in Patna, said: "We are of the view that any attempt to tarnish the image of national heroes should not be permitted." In truth, the film reveals Gandhi's humanity and that, says [his great-grandson] Tushar Gandhi, should have been exposed a long time ago. "Gandhi has become a hostage to his mahatmaship. It is easy to say that we cannot emulate someone like him when we put him on a pedestal. What we should be doing is seeing him as a normal, frail human being who strove to achieve something. We should emulate people like him, but not worship them."

Sarfraz Manzoor, *The Guardian*, August 10, 2007

⁵⁰ **renunciation** giving up
⁵¹ **to gratify** to indulge in
⁵³ **to espouse** *(fml)* to adopt and support (a belief)
⁶⁰ **poignant** causing a feeling of sadness
⁶⁰ **an inconvenient truth** *here:* a reality people find hard to accept (play on the title of a film about climate change)
⁷¹ **to stem from** to be caused by
⁷⁴ **partial to** showing a preference for
⁷⁷ **fragile** easy to break
⁸³ **to tarnish** *beflecken*
⁸⁶ **hostage** *Geisel*
⁸⁶ **mahatmaship** (invented noun) state of being a 'mahatma'
⁸⁷ **to emulate** to try to be as good as or better than

1 Describe and evaluate the conflict between Gandhi and his eldest son.

2 a) [👥👥👥] *Discuss what sources of information you would use and how you would present a figure of historical importance in a film. Take notes.*
   b) [👥👥] *Use your notes to prepare and act out a dialogue between Khan and one of the people who protested against his film.*
   c) [👥👥👥] *Write a scene for a film in which Harilal and his father are having an argument. Act it out and record it, then present it to the class.*

> **WORD BANK**
>
> **talking about contrasts**
> on the one/the other hand • a huge discrepancy between • whereas/while • to have little/nothing in common with • unlike • as opposed to • at odds with • the reverse of

2 The wounds of history

[Online-Link: **601006-0008**]

Cracking India

The narrator in Bapsi Sidhwa's novel Cracking India, *an 8-year-old girl called Lenny, lives in Lahore with her affluent and well-educated Parsee family. She has a habit of making up fantasy names for people and things she likes.*

There is much disturbing talk. India is going to be broken. Can one break a country? And what happens if they break it where our house is? Or crack it further up on Warris Road? How will I ever get to Godmother's then? I ask Cousin. "Rubbish," he says, "no one's going to break India. It's not made of glass!" I ask Ayah. "They'll dig a canal …," she ventures. "This side for Hindustan and this side for Pakistan. If they want two countries that's what they'll have to do – crack India with a long, long canal." Gandhi, Jinnah, Nehru, Iqbal, Tara Singh, Mountbatten are names I hear. And I become aware of religious differences.

It is sudden. One day everybody is themselves – and the next they are Hindu, Muslim, Sikh, Christian. People shrink, dwindling into symbols. Ayah is no longer just my all-encompassing Ayah – she is also a token. A Hindu. Carried away by a renewed devotional fervor she expends a small fortune in joss-sticks, flowers and sweets on the gods and goddesses in the temples. Imam Din and Yousaf, turning into religious zealots, warn Mother they will take Friday off for the Jumha prayers. On Fridays they set about preparing themselves ostentatiously. Squatting atop the cement wall of the garden tank they hold their feet out beneath the tap and diligently scrub between their toes. They wash their heads, arms, necks and ears and noisily clear their throats and noses. All in white check prayer scarves thrown over their shoulders, stepping uncomfortably in stiff black Bata shoes worn without socks, they walk out of the gates to the small mosque at the back of Queens Road. Sometimes, at odd hours of the day, they spread their mats on the front lawn and pray when the muezzin calls. Crammed into a narrow religious slot they too are diminished, as are Jinnah and Iqbal, Ice-candy-man and Masseur. Hari and Moti-the-sweeper and his wife Muccho, and their untouchable daughter Papoo, become even more untouchable as they are entrenched deeper in their low Hindu caste. While the Sharmas and the Daulatrams, Brahmins like Nehru, are dehumanized by their lofty caste and caste-marks.

The Rogers of Birdwood Barracks, Queen Victoria and King George are English Christians: they look down their noses upon the Pens who are Anglo-Indian, who look down upon all non-Christians. Godmother, Slavesister, Electric-aunt and my nuclear family are reduced to irrelevant nomenclatures – we are Parsee. What is God?

From: Bapsi Sidhwa, *Cracking India*, 1991

VIP FILE

Bapsi Sidhwa, born in 1938, a Parsee (member of a very powerful religious group in India) from Karachi raised in Lahore, lives in Houston/ Texas today and is one of Pakistan's most acclaimed diasporic writers. Her novel *Cracking India* (1991) was made into the award-winning film *Earth* (1998) by director Deepa Mehta, who called this film her "antiwar statement".

---

⁵ **ayah** nanny
¹¹ **token** symbol
¹² **devotional fervor** religious passion
¹⁴ **zealot** ['zelət] fanatic
¹⁵ **Jumha prayers** congregational Friday prayers
²⁰ **Bata** brand name
²⁷ **lofty** exalted, superior

TIP
Research on the Internet which role *Nehru, Iqbal* and *Tara Singh* played in the Partition of India and give a short presentation.

---

1 *Make a grid with the names of all the people mentioned in this extract, noting down who/what they are and how Partition affects them.*

2 *How does Lenny feel about Partition and its effects on the people around her? Interpret her question in the last line.*

3 [👥] ***Creative writing:*** *Imagine you were a Hindu and your best friend a Muslim. After Partition you live on separate sides of the border. Write a letter to express your feelings about Partition. Then read each other's texts and discuss their quality and content.*

Spot on facts

Indian independence

British expansion in India, from the earliest activities of the East India Company to the establishment of the Raj, was achieved by military power in the face of considerable local resistance. Consequently, unrest and opposition to British rule were a permanent undercurrent that surfaced from time to time, most notably in the Indian Rebellion of 1857. This began as a mutiny of Indian soldiers in the British Army and spread to other sections of the population.

With the founding of the Indian National Congress in 1885 the desire for Indian independence took on a more organised form. Initially the Congress merely sought more rights for the Indian population under British rule using the moderate means of prayer, petition and protest. However, by the early 1900s many within the party advocated a more radical and militant approach and boycotts of British goods were organised and there were outbreaks of violence.

The Congress was predominantly Hindu and the Muslim population did not feel represented by it. This led to the founding of the Muslim League in 1906, giving the British, who had no intention of granting Indian independence, the opportunity to stall nationalist demands by playing the two parties off against each other.

The nationalist movement grew throughout the 20s and 30s especially under the leadership of Gandhi, who was able to inspire the masses to follow his strategy of non-violent civil disobedience.

By 1946 the crippling effect of the Second World War, the heightened nationalistic feeling in the Indian population and, crucially, the mutiny by sailors of the Royal Indian Navy had all combined to bring home to the British that holding onto India would be impossible. The problem was how to withdraw without leaving chaos in their wake. The Hindus wanted a united independent India. The Muslims, afraid of Hindu domination, had long been demanding the creation of a separate nation, Pakistan. To resolve the deadlock, the British came up with plans for a "three-tier federation for India", which would divide the region into three groups of provinces with the Hindu-populated provinces making up Group A and the largely Muslim-populated ones in Groups B and C. The idea found no acceptance. For the Hindus it went too far, for the Muslims not far enough. The Sikhs of the Punjab found themselves in Group B and wanted their own nation-state. The result was rioting and bloodshed between the religious groups as well as mass migration from province to province, which continued after the withdrawal of the British and the creation of the two independent states of India and Pakistan.

1. *Explain the relationship between the British, the Indian National Congress and the Muslim League in the decades before Partition and point out what finally led to the British withdrawal.*

2. a) [🖥] *Find out about the two parts of Pakistan and what happened to them.*
   b) [🖥] *Research the Prime Ministers of India since 1947 and comment on your findings.*

2 The wounds of history

Exit Wounds – The legacy of Indian Partition

In his article 'Exit Wounds' Pankaj Mishra expresses his thoughts about Partition.

Sixty years ago, on the evening of August 14, 1947, a few hours before Britain's Indian Empire was formally divided into the nation-states of India and Pakistan, Lord Louis Mountbatten and his wife, Edwina, sat down in the viceregal mansion in New Delhi to watch the latest Bob Hope movie, 'My Favorite Brunette'. Large parts of the subcontinent were descending into chaos, as the implications of partitioning the Indian Empire along religious lines became clear to the millions of Hindus, Muslims, and Sikhs caught on the wrong side of the border. In the next few months, some twelve million people would be uprooted and as many as a million murdered. But on that night in mid-August the bloodbath – and the fuller consequences of hasty imperial retreat – still lay in the future, and the Mountbattens probably felt they had earned their evening's entertainment.

Mountbatten, the last viceroy of India, had arrived in New Delhi in March, 1947, charged with an almost impossible task. Irrevocably enfeebled by the Second World War, the British belatedly realized that they had to leave the subcontinent, which had spiralled out of their control through the nineteen-forties. But plans for brisk disengagement ignored messy realities on the ground. Mountbatten had a clear remit to transfer power to the Indians within fifteen months. Leaving India to God, or anarchy, as Mohandas Gandhi, the foremost Indian leader, exhorted, wasn't a political option, however tempting. Mountbatten had to work hard to figure out how and to whom power was to be transferred.

The dominant political party, the Congress Party, took inspiration from Gandhi in claiming to be a secular organization, representing all four hundred million Indians. But many Muslim politicians saw it as a party of upper-caste Hindus and demanded a separate homeland for their hundred million co-religionists, who were intermingled with non-Muslim populations across the subcontinent's villages, towns, and cities. Eventually, as in Palestine, the British saw partition along religious lines as the quickest way to the exit. But sectarian riots in Punjab and Bengal dimmed hopes for a quick and dignified British withdrawal, and boded ill for India's assumption of power. Not surprisingly, there were some notable absences at the Independence Day celebrations in New Delhi on August 15th. Gandhi, denouncing freedom from imperial rule as a "wooden loaf", had remained in Calcutta, trying, with the force of his moral authority, to stop Hindus and Muslims from killing each other. His great rival Mohammed Ali Jinnah, who had fought bitterly for a separate homeland for Indian Muslims, was in Karachi, trying to hold together the precarious nation-state of Pakistan. […]

Cyril Radcliffe, a London barrister, was flown to Delhi and given forty days to define precisely the strange political geography of an India flanked by an eastern

---

[8] **uprooted** deprived of one's roots
[10] **retreat** withdrawal
[13] **enfeebled** weakened
[17] **remit** *(fml)* task
[23] **secular** not religious
[30] **to bode ill** to suggest that sth bad will happen
[36] **precarious** unstable, dangerous
[37] **barrister** lawyer

The wounds of history

and a western wing called Pakistan. He did not visit the villages, communities,
40 rivers, or forests divided by the lines he drew on paper. Ill-informed about the relation between agricultural hinterlands and industrial centers, he made a mistake of enormous economic consequence when, dividing Bengal on religious lines, he deprived the Muslim majority in the eastern region of its major city, Calcutta, condemning East Pakistan – and, later, Bangladesh – to decades of
45 rural backwardness.

It was in Punjab that Radcliffe's mapmaking sparked the biggest conflagration. As Hindus, Muslims, and Sikhs on either side of the new border suddenly found themselves reduced to a religious minority, the tensions of the preceding months exploded into the violence of ethnic cleansing. It seems
50 extraordinary today that so few among the cabal of Indian leaders whom Mountbatten consulted anticipated that the drawing of borders and the crystallizing of national identities along religious lines would plunge millions into bewilderment, panic, and murderous rage. If the British were eager to divide and quit, their successors wanted to savor power. No one had prepared for a
55 massive transfer of population. Even as armed militias roamed the countryside, looking for people to kidnap, rape, and kill, houses to loot, and trains to derail and burn, the only force capable of restoring order, the British Indian Army, was itself being divided along religious lines – Muslim soldiers to Pakistan, Hindus to India. Soon, many of the communalized soldiers would join their co-religionists
60 in killing sprees, giving the violence of partition its genocidal cast.

Trains carrying nothing but corpses through a desolate countryside became the totemic image of the savagery of partition. British soldiers confined to their barracks, ordered by Mountbatten to save only British lives, may prove to be the most enduring image of imperial retreat. With this act of moral dereliction, the
65 British Empire finally disowned its noble sense of mission. As Paul Scott put it in [his novel] 'The Raj Quartet', the epic of imperial exhaustion and disillusion, India in 1947 was where the empire's high idea of itself collapsed and "the British came to the end of themselves as they were."

Meeting Mountbatten a few months after partition, Churchill assailed him
70 for helping Britain's "enemies", "Hindustan" against "Britain's friends", the Muslims. Little did Churchill know that his expedient boosting of political Islam would eventually unleash a global jihad engulfing even distant New York and London. The rival nationalisms and politicized religions the British Empire brought into being now clash in an enlarged geopolitical arena; and the human
75 costs of imperial overreaching seem unlikely to attain a final tally for many more decades.

Pankaj Mishra, *The New Yorker*, August 13, 2007

VIP FILE

Pankaj Mishra, born 1969 in North India, is a writer, literary critic and lecturer, living in Mashobra and London. In his novels and essays he portrays crucial political and social developments on the Indian subcontinent.

---

⁴⁵**rural** *(adj)* referring to life away from town
⁴⁷**conflagration** fire
⁵⁰**cabal** a group of people meeting secretly
⁵²**to plunge** *here:* to drive
⁵³**bewilderment** confusion
⁶⁰**spree** short period of doing sth excessively
⁶⁹**to assail** to attack
⁷¹**expedient** useful in a particular situation
⁷⁵**tally** a record of amount

---

1 Summarise why Partition seemed inevitable to the people in power in 1947.

2 Point out what mistakes Mishra believes the British to have made in the process of quitting India and how he judges the consequences, both nationally and internationally. Be careful to distinguish between fact and opinion, and discuss Mishra's views.

3 Analyse how Mountbatten, Radcliffe and Churchill are presented in the text.

4 Imagine the article were to be included in an anthology published on the occasion of the 60th anniversary of Indian independence and write an introductory paragraph for it.

WORD BANK

to maintain law and order • multicultural society • tensions between ethnic/religious groups • ethnic cleansing • genocidal – genocide • to disregard • economic factors • to take over responsibility • benefit • to reach a political solution • to negotiate • to result in

2 The wounds of history

Muslims – India's new 'untouchables'

The following article was written in reaction to a coordinated series of terrorist attacks in Mumbai from 26–29 November 2008. One of the locations targeted was the Taj Mahal Palace & Tower Hotel.

The news of the attacks in Mumbai eerily took me back to a quiet morning two years ago when I sat in Room 721 of the Taj Mahal Palace & Tower Hotel, reading the morning newspaper, fearing just the kind of violence that has now exploded in the city of my birth. The headlines recounted how the socioeconomic condition of the people of my ancestry, Muslims in India, had fallen below that of the Hindu caste traditionally called 'untouchables', according to a government report.

"Muslims are India's new untouchables", I said sadly to my mother, in the room with me. "India is going to explode if it doesn't take care of them." Now, indeed, alas it has. And shattered in the process is the myth of India's thriving secular democracy.

Mumbai police said over the weekend that the only gunman they'd captured during the attacks – which left nearly 200 dead and more than 300 wounded – claimed to belong to a Pakistani militant group. But even if the trouble was imported, the violence will most certainly turn a spotlight of suspicion on Muslims in India. Already, my relatives are hunkered down for a sectarian backlash they expect from anti-terrorism agencies, police and angry Hindu fundamentalists.

India, long championed as a model of pluralism, used to be an example of how Muslims can coexist and thrive even as a minority population. My extended family prospered as part of an educated middle class. My parents, who settled in the United States in the 1960s when my father pursued a doctorate at Rutgers University, were part of India's successful diaspora. I love India, and on that trip, I wanted to show it off to my son, Shibli, then age 4.

But on that visit, across India from Mumbai to the southern state of Tamil Nadu and north to Lucknow, the hub of Muslim culture, I was deeply saddened. Talking to vegetable vendors, artisans and businessmen, I heard about how the condition of Muslims had deteriorated. They had become largely disenfranchised, poor, jobless and uneducated. Their tales echoed those I'd heard on previous trips, when my extended family recounted their humiliating experiences with bureaucratic, housing, job and educational discrimination.

Indeed, the government report I read about in the newspapers two years ago acknowledged that Muslims in India had become "backward". "Fearing for their security," the report said, "Muslims are increasingly resorting to living in ghettos around the country." Branding of Muslims as anti-national, terrorists and agents of Pakistan "has a depressing effect on their psyche," the report said, noting Muslims live in "a sense of despair and suspicion".

According to the report, produced by a committee led by a former Indian chief justice, Rajender Sachar, Muslims were now worse off than the Dalit caste, or those called untouchables. Some 52% of Muslim men were unemployed, compared with 47% of Dalit men. Among Muslim women, 91% were unemployed, compared with 77% of Dalit women. Almost half of Muslims over the age of 46 couldn't read or write. While making up 11% of the population, Muslims accounted for 40% of India's prison population. Meanwhile, they held less than 5% of government jobs.

A poor Muslim quarter

The Taj Mahal Hotel after the terrorist attacks in 2008

¹**eerie** strange and frightening
⁴**to recount** to tell
¹⁰**alas** expression of regret
¹⁰**to thrive** to grow healthily
¹⁶**to hunker down** to get into a low (defensive) position
¹⁷**backlash** negative reaction
²¹**to prosper** to do well financially
²⁹**to disenfranchise** to deprive of rights
³¹**humiliating** causing loss of dignity publicly

The Sachar committee report recommended creating a commission to remedy the systemic discrimination and promote affirmative-action programs. So far, very few of the recommendations have been put in place.

Since reading the report, I have feared that Islamic militancy would be born out of such despair. Even if last week's terrorist plot was hatched outside India, a cycle of sectarian violence could break out in the country and push some disenfranchised Muslim youth to join militant groups using hot-button issues like Israel and Kashmir as inspiration.

What has irked me these last years is how the world has glossed over India's problems. In 2006, for instance, former U.S. Defense Secretary William Cohen, whose Cohen Group invests heavily in India, said the U.S. and India were "perfect partners" because of their "multiethnic and secular democracies". When I asked to interview Cohen about the socioeconomic condition of Muslims, his public relations staffer said that conversation was too "in the weeds". But, to me, the condition of Muslims needs frank and open discussion if there is to be any hope of stemming Islamic radicalism and realizing true secular democracy in the country.

India's 150 million Muslims represent the second-largest Muslim population in the world, smaller only than Indonesia's 190 million Muslims. That is just bigger than Pakistan's 140 million Muslims or the entire population of Arab Muslims, which numbers about 140 million. U.S. intelligence reports continually warn that economic, social and political discontent are catalysts for radicalism, so we would be naive to continue to ignore this potential threat to the national security not just of India but the United States.

Throughout my 2006 journey, I found the idea of India's potential for danger unavoidable. On one leg, my son tucked safely in bed with my mother in our Taj hotel room, I went out to watch the filming of *A Mighty Heart*, the movie about the murder of Wall Street Journal reporter Daniel Pearl by Muslim militants in Pakistan. When the location scouts needed to replicate the treacherous streets of Karachi's militant Islamic culture, they didn't have to go far. They found the perfect spot in a poor Muslim neighborhood of Mumbai.

Asra Q. Nomani, *Los Angeles Times*, December 1, 2008

An anti-India protest rally in Islamabad to mark the Kashmir Solidarity Day

⁴⁸**to remedy** to put right a bad or wrong situation
⁵¹**plot** *here:* secret plan to do sth illegal or harmful
⁵¹**to hatch** *here:* to plan
⁵⁵**to irk** to annoy
⁵⁵**to gloss over** to try to hide by dealing with too briefly
⁶⁰**in the weeds** *here:* difficult to find time for
⁶²**to stem** to stop or restrict
⁷²**leg** section of a journey
⁷²**tucked** *here:* under the bedclothes
⁷⁵**location scout** person who looks for places to film
⁷⁶**treacherous** having hidden or unpredictable dangers

1 Explain the heading of the article. Collect the information given to support this idea and present it in a suitable way, e.g. using visualising techniques.

2 Pick out references the writer makes to her own personal feelings. Explain and comment on the context of these emotions.

3 If necessary using a dictionary to help you, paraphrase these expressions: a spotlight of suspicion (line 15); diaspora (line 23); affirmative-action programs (line 48); hot-button issues (line 53).)

4 [🖥] [👥] Find out on the Internet why Kashmir is an issue for militant Islamists.

5 Discuss to what extent you think a country should be left to solve its own problems without pressure or influence from other countries.

6 *Creative writing:* Look again at the 2007 article by Dr Shashi Tharoor on pages 6/7. Think how Asra Q. Nomani might have reacted to the article at the time. Write a letter from her to the newspaper giving her comments.

> **WORD BANK**
> **Disagreeing politely in a formal letter**
> With the greatest respect, … • I would like to voice the opinion that … • While conceding that … • Surely it cannot be denied that … • I feel obliged to point out that … • Unfortunately I cannot fully accept …

1 *While reading:* Note down the main ideas in each paragraph to help you understand how the author structures and develops his theme.

Looking across the border

To many Indians, the very existence of Pakistan is seen as a dagger aimed at the heart of India. This threat is perceived on a number of levels. First, Pakistan claims Kashmir, India's only Muslim-majority province. Pakistan is unlikely to relinquish that claim, precisely because it is majority Muslim. If the so-called 'two-nation' theory (which Jinnah propounded) is wrong then Pakistan should never have been created. If it is right then Kashmir should belong to Pakistan. Given the degree to which Pakistan's military regimes have demanded national sacrifice in both blood and capital in pursuit of the Kashmiri cause, it would be surprising if Islamabad abandoned its stance.

Second, the creation of Pakistan was seen as an amputation of India's natural geographical and cultural boundaries. It is not only the Hindu nationalists who dream of the day when Pakistan will be reincorporated into Akhand Bharat – Greater India. Many Indians, of whatever background, see partition as an unnecessary tragedy that ought, at some unspecified stage in the future, to be peacefully rectified. Naturally, this attitude contributes to Pakistan's own profound insecurities. However, very few Indians would any longer subscribe to Nehru's view that Pakistan was untenable as a nation state and that it would eventually merge back into India. Indian longing for subcontinental unity remains a vague sentiment. It is not a policy.

Third, and most intractably, Pakistan is seen as posing an existential threat to India's secular identity. No matter how stable relations are between the two countries, in the Indian mind the existence of Pakistan will always have the potential to divide the loyalties of India's Muslim minority, which now accounts for almost 14 per cent of the population, or about 150 million people. This, in turn, exacerbates the insecurities of India's Muslims. There is little doubt that Pakistan has on many occasions over the last sixty years sought to stoke this neuralgia. Yet, with the exception of Kashmir, which accounts for less than 10 per cent of India's Muslim population, the expectations of many in Pakistan (and around the world) that India would gradually break up under the weight of its diverse contradictions have been proved wrong. India's Muslims remain firmly ensconced in India, as do most of India's other minorites. There have been no significant population movements between India and Pakistan since 1947. […]

Someone once said that the rivalry between the Soviet Union and the United States during the Cold War was ideological, whereas the enmity between India and Pakistan is biological. Whenever I visit Pakistan, I am struck by the transparent paranoia that the military and diplomatic elites in Islamabad feel towards their neighbour. I am equally struck by the absence of these sentiments among ordinary Pakistanis. The same is broadly true in reverse, although India plays a much larger role in the popular perceptions of Pakistanis than vice versa, partly because of the allure of Bollywood. When ordinary Pakistanis and Indians interact there is usually goodwill and warmth.

From: Edward Luce, *In Spite of the Gods*, 2006

[4] **to relinquish** to give up
[5] **to propound** to put forward (an idea or theory)
[9] **stance** *here:* viewpoint
[17] **to subscribe to** to agree with
[20] **intractable** resistant to good arguments or reasons
[25] **to exacerbate** to make (a problem) worse
[31] **to ensconce** to establish (in a place)

2 [2️⃣] *The India-Pakistan border is closed every evening. Before watching the video, say what you expect this event to be like. After viewing, describe the closing of the border in detail and compare it with your expectations.*

The wounds of history | 2

3 *Refer to the text and the film to compare and contrast the view across the India-Pakistan border from both sides. Consider the perspective both at government level and of private individuals.*

4 *The text below is a report on one aspect of the consequences of the November 2008 terrorist attacks in Mumbai. Sum up the main points in English for an Indian friend who is interested in how events in India are seen in Europe.*

5 a) *Comment on the contents of the Spiegel article in the light of what Edward Luce writes about the relationship between India and Pakistan.*
   b) *What other examples do you know of tensions between neighbouring countries? Research the necessary information and give a short presentation.*

Indische Presse bezichtigt Pakistans Geheimdienst der Terrorhilfe

Neu Delhi – Die Spannungen zwischen Indien und Pakistan nach den blutigen Anschlägen von Mumbai haben eine neue Dimension erreicht: Indien hat nach Zeitungsberichten angeblich Beweise dafür, dass der pakistanische Geheimdienst in die Anschläge in der indischen Finanzmetropole verwickelt ist. Indische Sicherheitsbehörden gingen […] davon aus, dass der pakistanische Geheimdienst ISI eine aktive Rolle bei der Ausbildung der Angreifer gespielt habe, berichteten mehrere indische Zeitungen am Freitag.

Die Details zu den Vorwürfen sind allerdings denkbar nebulös. In keiner der Zeitungen werden Quellen namentlich genannt, stattdessen zitieren die Blätter Spekulationen unter Berufung auf anonyme Behördenmitarbeiter. Zum Beispiel: Den Ermittlern sei bekannt, wer die Terroristen trainiert habe, die vorige Woche während der 60 Stunden andauernden Terrorwelle mehr als 170 Menschen töteten. Außerdem wisse man, wo das Kampftraining stattgefunden habe. Das berichten übereinstimmend die Zeitungen „Hindustan Times", „Indian Express" und „The Hindu". Namen oder Orte werden allerdings nicht genannt.

Die Terroristen hätten außerdem bestimmte Kommunikationswege per Voice-over-IP benutzt, die auch der ISI verwendet – den Berichten zufolge ein Beweis dafür, dass die Geheimdienstler den Terroristen halfen. […]

Zudem, so wollen die ominösen Quellen in Erfahrung gebracht haben, müsse das Militär über die Terrorpläne des ihm unterstellten Geheimdienstes Bescheid gewusst haben. Die zivile Regierung Pakistans hingegen war demnach angeblich ahnungslos. Das werten die Beobachter als weiteren Hinweis darauf, dass die Spannungen zwischen dem mächtigen Militär und der gewählten Regierung des Landes äußerst groß sind.

Lediglich einer der Attentäter konnte verhaftet werden. Neun weitere wurden getötet. […] Der Verhaftete habe ausgesagt, in den vergangenen anderthalb Jahren an vier Schulungen in Ausbildungslagern in Pakistan teilgenommen zu haben, berichtete die Zeitung „Mail Today". Er gehöre der Lashkar-i-Toiba an, der bereits mehrere Anschläge in Indien zur Last gelegt werden. Die islamistische Gruppe kämpft gegen die indische Herrschaft im umstrittenen Kaschmir-Gebiet. Ihr wurden schon in der Vergangenheit Beziehungen zum pakistanischen Geheimdienst nachgesagt. […]

Spiegel Online, 5. Dezember, 2008

> **FACT FILE**
> The Islamic Republic of Pakistan has a history of both military and civilian rule. Having come to power in a coup in 1999, General Pervez Musharraf declared a nominal democracy in 2001, but while President also remained head of the military. In February 2008 parliamentary elections restored a civilian government which was in power at the time of the terrorist attacks in Mumbai.

[6] ISI Inter Services Intelligence Agency

Topic 3   Different worlds

>> I am convinced that if India is to attain true freedom, and through India the world also, then sooner or later the fact must be recognised that people will have to live in villages, not towns; in huts, not in palaces. Crores of people will never be able to live in peace with each other in towns and palaces. They will then have no recourse but to resort to both violence and untruth. <<

Mahatma Gandhi, in a letter to Jawahrlal Nehru

WORD BANK
Talking about lifestyles
standard of living • to live below the poverty line • to eke out a living • to be well-off • affluence • good/poor quality housing • slums • access to services • (lack of) amenities • secure/casual employment • consumer lifestyle • hectic/slow pace of life • to flaunt one's wealth

1. a) *Outline what the photos tell you about rural and urban life in India. Focus especially on the contrasts you notice, commenting on aspects that make a particular impression on you in some way.*
   b) *Suggest captions for the photos, summarising and interpreting the information they convey.*

2. Use the visual information together with the statistics above to collect ideas about why the rural-urban divide is a problem for India. Think about factors such as: economic productivity; infrastructure; health and education; conflicting demands on the water supply; migration.

Different worlds 3

>> The love of the intellectual Indian for the village community is of course infinite, if not pathetic … What is the village but a sink of localism, a den of ignorance, narrow mindedness and communalism? <<

Bhimrao Ambedkar (1891–1956), Dalit leader and main author of India's 1950 constitution, which gives legal equality to all individuals regardless of caste

Statistics
- Only 27.8% of Indians live in cities, but their contribution to the national economy is 60%.
- More than 100 million rural Indians do not own any land.
- The 65% of the population who depend on agriculture for a living contribute only 25% to the total economy.
- Between 1991 and 2001 over 70 million people migrated from rural areas to cities.
- India has 17% of the world's population but only 4% of its fresh water.
- Domestic water use in urban areas is expected to double by 2025, and industrial use is expected to triple.
- 40% of all Indian families live in one-room houses.
- 50% of people in Mumbai live in shanty towns, in open spaces in the city or on pavements.
- It is estimated that there are 150,000 street children in Delhi.
- The national male literacy rate is 75.9% while the rate for females is 54.2%.

3 a) *Read the two quotations above and compare the attitudes expressed towards the concept of village life. Relate Gandhi's words to what you already know about him. Sum up how the information given about Ambedkar helps to explain his views.*
   b) *Some people argue that despite Gandhi's achievements he has also been a negative influence on India. Try to explain why.*

4 a) *[4◉] Listen to Mark Tully talking about the lifestyle of a poor man in Calcutta. Describe what job the man does, where he lives and what the conditions are like.*
   b) *What does Tully say about the man's attitude towards his fate in life and why he thinks it would be dangerous to talk to him about it? Discuss whether you agree with Tully.*

crores *(Hindi)* tens of millions
communalism *here:* allegiance to one's own ethnic and social group

> **TIP**
> At the beginning of the track Tully refers to 'Dickens'. If you don't know who this is, find out!

3   Different worlds

A meeting of the Children's Parliament of Tilonia

FACT FILE
Suttee was discouraged by Indians wanting to reform society even long before the British made it illegal in 1829. Although it is very rare in modern India, cases do still occur. Because of the cult status of the practice, women who commit suttee attract followers, and memorials to them exist all over India.

1 a) [3▶] *Watch the video once without taking notes. Sum up who the Barefoot College is for and what its main aim is.*
   b) *Watch again and collect the information you need to answer these questions.*
      1. *What is the Children's Parliament and how does it work?*
      2. *What kind of skills do you see women being taught, and why?*
      3. *In what ways is the Barefoot College community different from traditional rural Indian society?*
   c) [🖥] *Research: Look up the Barefoot College on the Internet to find out more about it and the problems it addresses.*

2 *Before reading:* India's constitution gives women the same legal rights as men, but as mentioned in the Barefoot college video, gender inequality remains a problem. Speculate on how this kind of discrimination might affect females at different stages of their life.

3 *Skim the text for the gist and give your immediate reaction.*

'Long live Suttee' cried the mob

On the evening of August 5 Mallu Nai, a poor barber in rural India, died at home in his simple mud hut.

There was nothing unusual about his death: he was 60, a good age by Indian standards, and had been ill for some time. Early the next morning, his widow, Kuttu Bai, got up and put on her old wedding sari. She then, apparently, announced her intention to commit suttee – the ancient practice in which an Indian widow burns herself to death on her husband's funeral pyre.

As word of Kuttu's impending sacrifice spread, some 2,000 villagers gathered to watch. The 65-year-old widow walked from her home to a nearby hillock and her husband's funeral pyre and sat down on it. The crowd lit incense sticks and made offerings of coconuts. They also fed her betel leaves, the local crop. The widow cradled her husband's head in her lap.

There is strong evidence that Kuttu was alive and sitting on the pyre for two hours before her elder son, Ashok, finally set light to it. Then two local police constables arrived. Senior officers claim that one of them, Harcharan Singh, tried to drag Kuttu off the blazing pyre but was beaten back by the mob who pelted him with stones. Other sources say that the policemen simply ran away.

As Kuttu keeled over, the mob shouted: "Suttee mata ki jai" or "Long live Suttee, our mother". They were the last words Kuttu heard before her body was reduced to ashes, and her sad story became the stuff of controversy and myth.

Suttee goes back an entire millennium in India and is rooted in a Hindu belief that a widow gains god-like status by dying with her husband. But why did Kuttu Bai do it? And, more to the point, why did nobody from her village try to stop her?

The clues can be found in Tamoli itself, which lies in a poor and backward district in the northern state of Madhya Pradesh. Most of the 700 or so households survive by growing betel leaf, the main ingredient of paan, India's favourite stimulant. Tamoli, with its nondescript huts set in an undulating landscape, is 250 miles from the nearest big city. Its statistics are bleak. The female literacy rate is 19 %. Few villagers have television. There is no running water and not much electricity. Money allocated for development has disappeared. Several other villages in the district are even worse off, local administrators admit – but there is no doubt that for most people in Tamoli

⁷**funeral pyre** pile of wood on which a body is burnt as part of a funeral ceremony
⁸**impending** happening in the very near future
¹⁰**incense** substance producing a sweet smell when burnt
¹¹**betel** plant used as a mild stimulant
¹⁷**to pelt with** to throw at (in order to attack)
¹⁸**to keel over** to fall over on one side
²⁸**nondescript** with no special or interesting features
³¹**to allocate** to give for a specific purpose

staying alive is a daily struggle. Kuttu's family were at the bottom of the pile and
35 officially classed as BPL – below poverty line.
Kuttu lived separately from her husband, an unusual arrangement in an Indian village. The local collector, Ravindra Pastor, insists they were on poor terms. "The couple had been estranged. They had always quarrelled and had almost always lived separately."
40 Why, then, would she kill herself? Others say they were happily married. Kuttu also owned six acres of land – motive enough, the police speculated, for her sons to murder her. But a team from India's National Committee of Women who arrived in Tamoli three days afterwards concluded that nobody had forced her to do anything. "She wanted to kill herself. It wasn't because of pressure
45 from the family. The family wanted to stop her," Anusuiya Uike, a member of the delegation, says. "Suttee is a very shameful act."
It is hardly surprising that some women choose the perversely "empowering" option of suttee, given the miserable status of widows, Suan Visvanathan, a sociology lecturer at Jawaharlal Nehru University, Delhi, argues. Traditionally,
50 Hindu widows are not allowed to remarry; and, despite a century of reform, their lot is not an enviable one. "Widows are ostracised and not allowed to participate in rituals. She would have assumed her life would be one of isolation and despair and shame and suffering."
There are two Indias, she adds, a metropolitan India where 10 % of the
55 population is affluent, and a rural India where most people lead lives of medieval hardship.
The authorities have now deluged the area with literature preaching against suttee, a futile gesture since most people can't read. None of the villagers, meanwhile, are able to explain how Mallu's pyre was lit. Most say it caught fire
60 spontaneously, or with divine help. There is not much left of Kuttu Bai now: only a charred spot surrounded by incense sticks. Once the police depart, as they inevitably will, worshippers from across India will start to arrive.

Luke Harding, *Asian News*, November 1, 2002

[37] **collector** main government official in an area
[37] **to be on poor terms** to have a bad relationship
[51] **lot** a person's luck in life
[51] **enviable** causing other people to want the same
[51] **to ostracise** to exclude from society
[57] **to deluge** *here*: to give a huge quantity of sth
[58] **futile** useless, senseless
[61] **charred** made black by being burnt
[62] **to worship sb** to admire and to treat like a god

4 *Now look at the article again more closely. What information does it give about suttee and the possible reasons why Kuttu Bai committed suttee?*

5 a) [👥] *First talk about any discrepancies or contradictions you notice in the description of events. Then one partner makes a list of definite facts, and the other lists areas that are open to speculation.*
b) *Pick out words, phrases or devices which convey to the reader that the writer himself is not absolutely clear about what happened.*
c) *Summarise the results on the blackboard and discuss them. Has your opinion changed by dealing with the text in more detail?*

6 *Explain what is meant or implied by: a good age by Indian standards (line 3); the stuff of controversy and myth (line 20); its statistics are bleak (line 29); money allocated for development has disappeared (line 31); the perversely "empowering" option of suttee (line 47).*

7 **Discussion:** *Are westerners able to judge traditions or social systems in another country and culture?*

3 Different worlds

FACT FILE
80 % of the yearly rainfall in India occurs during the 4 months of the summer monsoon. The monsoon is unreliable, however, and sometimes the rains fail.

Hunger

That year the rains failed. A week went by, two. We stared at the cruel sky, calm, blue, indifferent to our need. We threw ourselves on the earth and we prayed. I took a pumpkin and a few grains of rice to my Goddess, and I wept at her feet. I thought she looked at me with compassion and I went away comforted, but no rain came.

"Perhaps tomorrow," my husband said. "It is not too late."

We went out and scanned the heavens, clear and beautiful, deadly beautiful, not one cloud to mar its serenity. Others did so, too, coming out, as we did, to gaze at the sky and murmur, "Perhaps tomorrow."

Tomorrows came and went and there was no rain. Nathan no longer said perhaps; only a faint spark of hope, obstinately refusing to die, brought him out each dawn to scour the heavens for a sign.

Each day the level of the water dropped and the heads of the paddy hung lower. The river had shrunk to a trickle, the well was as dry as a bone. Before long the shoots of the paddy were tipped with brown; even as we watched, the stain spread like some terrible disease, choking out the green that meant life to us.

Harvesting time, and nothing to reap. The paddy had taken all our labour and lay now before us in faded, useless heaps. […]

The drought continued until we lost count of the time. Day after day the pitiless sun blazed down, scorching whatever still struggled to grow and baking the earth hard until at last it split and great irregular fissures gaped in the land. Plants died and the grasses rotted, cattle and sheep crept to the river that was no more and perished there for lack of water, lizards and squirrels lay prone and gasping in the blistering sunlight.

In the town a water reservoir had been built for the tannery workers and their families, but now others were allowed a limited quantity as well. So thither I journeyed every morning, and, when I said how many we were, perhaps half a mud pot would be doled out, sometimes a little more, depending upon who was in charge. Then some of the women in their greed began to claim to have more children than they had, and non-existent relatives, and there were jealousies and spite and bitter argument. Until at last it was decreed that each person must come in his own right only, not for others, even children and old men, and this put an end to the cheating and quarrelling; but it was hard for many who had not their full strength.

Then, after the heat had endured for days and days, and our hopes had shrivelled with the paddy – too late to do any good – then we saw the storm clouds gathering, and before long the rain came lashing down, making up in fury for the long drought and giving the grateful land as much as it could suck and more. But in us there was nothing left – no joy, no call for joy. It had come too late.

As soon as the rains were over, and the cracks in the earth had healed, and the land was moist and ready, we took our seed to our Goddess and placed it at her feet to receive her blessing, and then we bore it away and made our sowing.

When a few weeks had gone by, the seed sprouted; tender shoots appeared, thrusting upwards with increasing strength, and soon we were able to transplant the seedlings one by one, and at first they stood out singly, slender, tremulous spires with spaces between: but grew and grew and soon were merged into one thick green field of rustling paddy. In that field, in the grain which had not yet begun to form, lay our future and our hope.

[2]**indifferent to** showing no interest in
[8]**to mar** to damage the appearance of
[8]**serenity** state of being calm and peaceful
[12]**to scour** *here:* to search
[13]**paddy** field where rice is grown
[15]**shoot** *Schößling*
[17]**to reap** to harvest a crop
[23]**to perish** to die
[23]**prone** lying face downwards
[24]**to gasp** to fight for breath
[25]**tannery** place where animal skins are made into leather
[26]**thither** *(archaic style)* to that place
[36]**to shrivel** to become dry and small
[42]**moist** damp
[43]**to sow** to place seed into the ground to make plants grow out of it
[44]**tender** *here:* easily injured
[45]**to thrust** to push
[46]**slender** elegantly slim
[47]**spire** tall, slim shape which narrows to a point
[47]**to merge** to join together

Different worlds

50   Hope, and fear. Twin forces that tugged at us first in one direction and then in another, and which was the stronger no one could say. Of the latter we never spoke, but it was always with us. Fear, constant companion of the peasant. Hunger, ever at hand to jog his elbow should he relax. Despair, ready to engulf him should he falter. Fear; fear of the dark future; fear of the sharpness of
55 hunger; fear of the blackness of death.

    Long before the paddy ripened we came to the end of our dried-fish stocks. There was no money left – every pie had gone to pay the land dues. Nothing left to sell. Nothing to be had from my efforts, for the vines and vegetables had withered in the long weeks of drought. […]
60   Thereafter we fed on whatever we could find: the soft ripe fruit of the prickly pear; a sweet potato or two, blackened and half-rotten, thrown away by some more prosperous hand; sometimes a crab that Nathan managed to catch near the river. Early and late my sons roamed the countryside, returning with a few bamboo shoots, a stick of sugar cane left in some deserted field, or a piece of
65 coconut picked from the gutter in the town. For these they must have ranged widely, for other farmers and their families, in like plight to ourselves, were also out searching for food; and for every edible plant or root there was a struggle – a desperate competition that made enemies of friends and put an end to humanity.
70   It was not enough. Sometimes from sheer rebellion we ate grass, although it always resulted in stomach cramps and violent retching. For hunger is a curious thing: at first it is with you all the time, waking and sleeping and in your dreams, and your belly cries out insistently, and there is a gnawing and a pain as if your very vitals were being devoured, and you must stop it at any cost, and you buy a
75 moment's respite even while you know and fear the sequel. Then the pain is no longer sharp but dull, and this too is with you always, so that you think of food many times a day and each time a terrible sickness assails you, and because you know this you try to avoid the thought, but you cannot, it is with you. Then that too is gone, all pain, all desire, only a great emptiness is left, like the sky,
80 like a well in drought, and it is now that the strength drains from your limbs, and you try to rise and find you cannot, or to swallow water and your throat is powerless, and both the swallow and the effort of retaining the liquid tax you to the uttermost.

    "It will not be long before the harvest," Nathan would murmur, and I would
85 agree with him, stifling the query whether our strength would last till then, saying, "Ah yes, not long now; only a little time before the grain is ripe."

From: Kamala Markandaya, *Nectar in a Sieve*, 1954

VIP FILE

Kamala Markandaya, 1924–2004; Indian journalist and novelist, whose fiction deals with issues such as poverty, rural-urban tension, gender.

50 **to tug** to pull
51 **the latter** the second (of two things or peope mentioned)
53 **to jog** *here:* to knock lightly
53 **to engulf** to swallow up
54 **to falter** to start to become weak or uncertain
57 **pie** unit of currency (no longer used)
57 **dues** payment that must be made for sth.
60 **prickly pear** type of cactus
62 **prosperous** wealthy
63 **to roam** to move around with no definite aim
65 **gutter** channel at the side of a street for carrying away rainwater
66 **plight** dangerous situation
71 **to retch** to be sick without being able to bring up anything from the stomach
73 **gnawing** *here:* constant pain
74 **very** *here:* themselves
74 **vitals** main internal organs
74 **to devour** to eat hungrily
75 **respite** short period of rest
75 **sequel** what follows
80 **limbs** arms and legs
82 **to tax** to require sb to use physical or mental powers
85 **to stifle** *here:* to suppress

1 a) *Create a diagram or flow chart showing how weather, actions, emotions and physical condition interact in the sequence described in the text.*
    b) *Comment on the exchange in the final paragraph.*

2 a) *Analyse how the author achieves such intensity in the style of the text.*
    b) *Prove that the text sounds biblical in many places by finding typical elements such as word fields, archaic vocabulary or word order, enumerations with "and" etc. How does this tone complement the content of the text?*

3 [👥] *Translation: Make a literary translation of lines 50–55. Compare and discuss versions with a partner.*

WORD BANK
Commenting on style
graphic description • use of repetition • alliteration • figurative language • to personify nature • simile • metaphor • archaic/poetic expression • sentence structure • word order • use of rhythm

3 Different worlds

VIP FILE

David Davidar, born 1959 in a town in Kerala, educated at Madras (Chennai) and Harvard, author and publisher, founding member of Penguin India, lives in Canada today and has written two novels so far.

[8] **guile** *(fml)* the quality of being good at deceiving people
[10] **on the cusp of** just before
[15] **audacious** daring
[16] **Chettiar** belonging to a trading community in South India
[20] **martinet** *(fml)* sb who believes in strict discipline
[24] **lashing** whipping
[25] **browbeaten** oppressed
[31] **depleted** run down
[33] **to come round** to change one's mind and agree with sth
[35] **closet communist** a communist in secret
[44] **mongrel** a dog with parents of different breeds
[47] **to exacerbate** [ɪɡˈzæsəbeɪt] to make a lot worse

The Solitude of Emperors

The narrator of this novel, which is set in the 1990s, is a young man called Vijay.

There were things in general that contributed to my disenchantment such as the lack of opportunity, the slow pace of life, the petty jealousies and small concerns of the people I associated with, but besides these there were specific things that stoked my desperation.

The first of these had little to do with me but with my parents and their romance. My mother taught physics at the women's college and my father economics at the government arts and science college I went to, and I felt they lacked the ambition and the guile to advance any further in their careers.

Or perhaps they were happy just as they were, muddling along with no real expectations in life, part of the generation of Indians born on the cusp of independence, with no big ideas to fight for, as the previous generation had had, and without the breathtaking ambition of succeeding generations. Their greatest achievement, as far as I could tell, because we didn't talk about such things, was getting married to one another. For they had married for love, and more audaciously across the caste divide – a titanic achievement in small-town India in 1967. My father was a Brahmin, and my mother belonged to the Chettiar caste, and they had attended the same college in Salem, their home town, where they had fallen in love. When they announced their intention to marry, my father's family promptly disowned him, and my mother's father, a thin-lipped old martinet who was the headmaster of a secondary school, and whose progressiveness extended only as far as letting his daughter attend college, locked her up in her room and began scheming with the extended family to send her to the most distant relative he could think of. For three days she had endured the lashings he administered with a belt, and then, in a plot line borrowed from Tamil cinema, she had sneaked out of the house – aided by her browbeaten mother – while her father had his afternoon siesta, wearing two saris and carrying a bottle of scented coconut oil and a large umbrella, the only things she could think of taking with her in the nerve-racking excitement of her escape. Soon after they were married in secret, the couple left Salem for K-, where they had lived quietly ever since. In my more charitable moments I would grant that the drama and tension of their marriage might have so depleted my parents that they had no option but to spend the rest of their lives just getting by.

My father's family eventually came round, especially after he assured them that I would be raised a good Brahmin, although he didn't intend to do much about it, a legacy of his having been a closet communist as a student. My mother's father never forgave her, not even when I arrived on the scene, which she'd hoped would be the occasion for at least a modest reconciliation. I never met my maternal grandfather as a result, and the few memories I have of my grandmother, who died a few years after her husband, are of a faded woman who dressed always in white, and took me to the Murugan temple every time we visited her in Salem.

My parents' crossing of caste lines had not only largely cut me off from my extended family – something that everyone else in town seemed to possess – it also marked me out as an oddity, a mongrel. It wasn't so bad because I was still a Brahmin and did not have to endure the various humiliations someone lower down the caste ladder would undoubtedly have to put up with, but I would never fit well into K-society. This was a condition somewhat exacerbated by my parents' unconventional attitude to religion. My father's brief flirtation with

Different worlds

communism had further diluted any lingering effects of his religious upbringing. I cannot remember him ever going to the temple in the years that my mother turned her back on religion, but neither did he believe in communism enough to delete religion entirely from his life. My mother, from whom I have inherited my stubbornness and a slow-burning temper, had been so enraged by her own family's treatment of her that she shut religion – which she blamed for her father's inflexibility – out of her existence and mine for the longest time. She allowed my mild-mannered father to fulfil his promise to his family by investing me with the sacred thread and other outward accoutrements of Brahminism, but beyond these token gestures I grew up without religion.

This, more than anything else, kept me from feeling completely at home in K-, for it was around caste and religion that the lives of its families and community revolved. In school and in college the Brahmin boys hung out together, the various non-Brahmin Hindus, depending on their numerical strength, formed their own groups, the Christian boys were separate, and had there been any Muslims in the educational institutions I studied in I have no doubt that they would have stayed within their own community. Most of the boys I knew went to the temple regularly and observed without question the myriad prohibitions and injunctions imposed upon them by the hierarchy of their faith. I was only tolerated, as I have said, because I was still an upper-caste Hindu. I faced numerous little indignities, none of them dramatic or interesting enough to dwell on, but over the years they deepened my sense of alienation, and made me even more eager to escape to the big cities where I'd heard you could do as you pleased, marry who you liked, go wherever you wanted. […]

In 1992 my journey, I thought, had finally begun. Bombay is not an attractive city. It has few tourist sights, its architecture is functional for the most part, the salt air from the Arabian Sea takes its toll on the most expensive buildings, and slums, noise, dense crowds, humidity, crime and pollution further deplete its charms. But it is one of the world's great cities with a vitality that defies belief, derived from the fourteen million people who call it home. I felt that charge from the minute my train deposited me in the early hours of the morning at VT station; all about me lay what looked like sheeted corpses, transients who slept on the railway platforms because they had nowhere else to go. I took a taxi to the hostel, an expensive luxury but unavoidable because of the enormous suitcase I was carrying, peering out of the window at the people who swarmed the streets, although it was barely light. These were my people, I thought; I was a Bombayite now. I could hardly wait to take the city by its throat. That didn't happen of course because, as I soon discovered, Bombay's sense of possibility and adventure was largely an illusion – none of the pretty girls who waited for the buses or the trains showed the least interest in me, no strangers walked up to me on the street and revealed mysterious worlds, but even as I scaled down my expectations the thrill of living in the city did not leave me.

From: David Davidar, *The Solitude of Emperors*, 2007

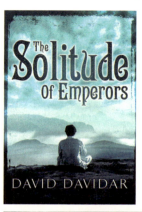

57 **accoutrement** symbol
67 **injunction** instruction
70 **to dwell on** to think or talk about sth a great deal
75 **to take its toll** to affect seriously
77 **to defy belief** [dɪˈfaɪ] to be hardly believable
80 **VT station** Victoria Terminus railway station
85 **to take sth by the throat** to make the most of an opportunity

1 Sum up the story of Vijay's parents and how he characterises them.

2 Compare the ways Vijay presents his hometown K- on the one hand and Bombay on the other with regard to his feelings, hopes and expectations.

TIP
Bombay = Mumbai
Calcutta = Kolkata
Madras = Chennai

33

Different worlds

A shocking transformation

The following text is a transcript of an interview with British Channel 4 television reporter and newsreader Krishnan Guru-Murthy, broadcast on April 30, 2007.

The story of the Indian economy is a real rags-to-riches story, isn't it?
Oh, it's a shocking transformation. The last time I went to India to spend time was five years ago, and the transformation between the India of 2002 and the India of 2007 is absolutely gob smacking. The cities have been totally transformed. Huge areas of land are being taken over by industrial parks, shopping malls everywhere. Huge, American-style malls are springing up literally next to each other. There's a road in Gurgaon, just outside Delhi, where you've literally got about six shopping malls right next to each other. They're full of people with money to spend, and all the western labels are there. It is shocking how much disposable income the new middle class has.

Where has the explosion in middle class wealth come from?
It's come about because the Indian boom has been very middle-class-knowledge-driven. We all know about call centres, but there's a huge amount of information technology, a lot of computer support stuff, a lot of software, and financial services and service industries growing up in India. That's put a huge amount of money in the hands of the middle classes. The time was in India when everyone wanted to be a professional – they wanted to be doctors, lawyers and accountants. Nobody wants to do that now, they all want to go into business, into the new technologies, because that's where the money is. […]

Does the new prosperity of the middle class put the poverty in India into even greater relief?
It's not so much the middle class as the super rich who really bring home to you the poverty of the poor in India. As well as the middle class explosion, there's been a creation of a new class of super-rich Indians. There are huge numbers of millionaires and billionaires in India now. We met a guy who had an ordinary upbringing, and turned a $10,000 investment ten years ago into a $2.5 billion business. So what you get in India is these extremes of wealth, and I think that puts the poverty and deprivation and the discrimination into much sharper relief.

Do you get the impression that the rich and the middle classes are distressed by the plight of the poor in India, or is it such an engrained part of life there that it no longer registers?
My own view is that Indians are very good at walking on by extreme poverty, not letting it trouble them too much. Partly because that's always been the way. If you spend your entire life worrying about the beggar or the guy who's living on the street, or the way your servant lives, you'd never get anything done in India. So Indians have a practical approach towards the poverty that they live alongside. But there's also a philosophical aspect that differs from the West. There is no guilt associated with being wealthy in India. In the West, in Judeo-Christian society, whether people are religious or not, there is basically a sense that it is easier for a camel to pass through the eye of a needle than it is for a rich man to enter the kingdom of heaven. There is no such concept in India. Hinduism encourages people to acquire wealth as part of their lives. […]

[4] **gob smacking** *(infml)* amazing
[7] **literally** without exaggeration
[12] **to come about** to happen
[20] **to put sth into relief** to make sth very clear (in contrast to sth else)
[22] **to bring home to** to make sb realise sth
[26] **upbringing** training and education as a child
[30] **distressed** very upset
[31] **engrained** deeply fixed
[43] **to acquire** to obtain

We're talking about a country of a billion people. How soluble are the problems of inequality?

I don't believe anything is insoluble. If, five years ago, you'd suggested to me that India would be the way it is today, I probably wouldn't have believed you. So rapid change can take place. The thing about India, though, as you say, is the scale. You have hundreds of millions of people who are going to have to change the way they live. Between 500 and 700 million people depend on agriculture in India. But agriculture is going to have to go through a massive change, from lots of small farms of two or three acres to more commercially sustainable, bigger farms that will make money. But that's going to mean hundreds of millions of people changing jobs. Whether that can happen very quickly, or whether it will take decades, is difficult to say. The Indian finance minister claims that India can rid itself of poverty within three decades. That is a very confident claim. But I'm not sure that that will answer the questions we're raising, about discrimination, caste, and what will happen to people living in the rural areas.

So what do you see as being the best case scenario for the future of India?

I think the best case scenario for India in the 21st century would be that it becomes one of the top three economies of the world, that it dramatically changes the lives of hundreds of millions of people in a generation, and becomes an economic superpower that also starts to demand its place on the world's political stage as well. From an Indian perspective, that is the dream.

And what's the worst case scenario?

That not enough of the new economy hits the whole of the country, and you get hundreds of millions of people in the rural areas who are landless and jobless. I talked to a hugely respected man called Swammimathan, who is described as the Father of the Green Revolution, which changed the way people farmed in the 1960s, and ended famine in India. He warned me that you could have 500 million landless labourers shut out of the new India, with the likelihood of social chaos and possible revolution. I don't really believe that there's going to be a revolution in India, but there is a real possibility of big problems trying to tackle these fundamental problems, and I think there's a real issue that you could end up with people at the bottom totally excluded. And in a country the size of India, you could be talking about hundreds of millions of people being shut out of the new India. And that can only lead to chaos.

From: *Channel 4 News*, 30 April, 2007

⁵²**sustainable** able to be maintained at a certain level
⁷⁰**famine** extreme lack of food
⁷³**to tackle** *here:* to deal with

1 a) *Outline what the text says about: 1. the changes that have taken place in India, 2. the reasons that lie behind these changes, 3. the Indian attitude towards wealth. Focus especially on the role of the middle class.*
  b) *Sum up the opinion expressed about what still needs to change, and why.*

2 a) [🎬] *Watch the video and compare the different perspectives of migrants and city dwellers. Why do people move to the city? How do city dwellers react to the incomers and what are their reasons?*
  b) *Point out the dangers and possibilities of mass migration to the cities.*

3 *Creative writing: Imagine the future of India and write an article in the year 2050. Choose either a best or a worst case scenario and describe the state of the country (think of economy, jobs, housing, health, education, equality etc.), explaining why it has developed in this way.*

WORD BANK

industrial park • shopping mall • disposable income • knowledge/…-driven • service industry • super rich • best/worst case scenario • economic superpower • the political stage • social chaos • fundamental problem

Topic 4   East meets West

The huge Indian diaspora includes 2.5 million people in the US and 1.5 million in the UK. Ties with the homeland usually remain close.

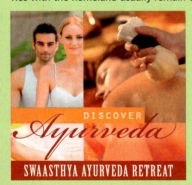

India's magic works wonders!

Western powers came to colonize the orient and ruled several countries in the east for centuries. The situation has come a full circle and dramatic changes are taking place in the East-West scenario. According to New York Times writer Thomas Friedman, US super brains are coming on a voyage to India in search of modern treasures. […] "Long centuries ago," he writes, "Columbus traveled eastward in search of 'hardware' – spices, silks and gold. Today's Columbus searches for treaures of another kind – 'software' like knowledge, services, ideas and concepts! Either way, India is rich!"

What Friedman says is a right-on-the-mark truth. With <u>men and women of Indian origin reaching top positions in the US</u> in education, business, research, fashion and art, India is truly shining in 2005! A few names deserve mention here. Indira Nuyi, Srinija Srinivasan and Padmasree Warrior head some of America's top companies. And now an alumnus of the Indian Institute of Management in Ahmedabad, Srikant Datar, is tipped to be the next dean of the prestigious Harvard Business School. Aside from academics, the Indian

5

10

15

West *here the term is basically limited to North America and Britain*
diaspora *here:* native Indians living outside India
¹⁴**dean** principal
²⁴**R** = rupee, Indian currency unit
²⁴**crore** *(Hindi)* ten million

WORD BANK
expatriate • to reside • outsourcing • offshoring • interdependence • to attract • education • globalisation

1 a) *Explain the idea expressed in the text that the contact between East and West has come a full circle.*
b) *In what areas has India made its mark in the West? What evidence of this do you see in your own country?*

2 a) *From what you have learned both about India's history and also about present-day India, find reasons for the huge number of Indians who have emigrated to the West.*
b) *Discuss the possible advantages and disadvantages for India of having such a large diaspora.*

East meets West 4

Many products sold in the west are sourced in India.

"You've come all this way seeking great wisdom, from someone who's stupid enough to sit half naked on top of a mountain?"

film industry or Bollywood also seems to have a huge footprint in the West. [...] Indian writers such as Salman Rushdie and Vikram Chandra are paid millions of dollars for their novels by US publishers. Indian food (Indian restaurants are winning every 'best' contest in the UK for years), fashion (international
20 designers are inviting Indian haute couture inventors to show their designs in Paris, Milan and London), lifestyle (Indian luxury goods like furniture, linen and carpets are flooding the eastern markets), weddings and jewellery (buyers and would-be brides are flocking to India for shopping) and art (M F Husain has just sold a painting for more than Rs.2 crores!) are impacting the West like never
25 before. The greatest exports of India today are culture, spiritualism, knowledge, art and other abstract qualities like exoticism and sensuality! India is fast becoming the medical, spiritual, adventure and exoticism-seeker tourists' Mecca and the number of visitors to India is galloping ahead.

From: Vimla Patil, *South Asian Women's Forum*, 2005

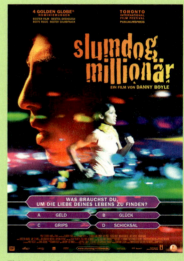

This multi-Oscar-winning movie was filmed in Mumbai

3 a) Share what you know about ayurveda and yoga, Indian food, music, films and literature.
   b) Discuss why you think so many westerners seem to be fascinated by Indian culture, philosophy and ideas.

4 Analyse and interpret the cartoon. What point is the cartoon making about the way in which westerners try to assimilate aspects of Indian culture?

5 Research: Find out about one of the successful Indians mentioned in the text above and give a short presentation.

WORD BANK
the lure of the exotic • out of the ordinary • holistic • to answer a need • sense of wellbeing • to be in stark contrast to • fusion of cultures • to tap into a market • the flavour of the month • to distort

37

4 East meets West

A family of Anglophiles

This text is an extract from the novel The God of Small Things. *The characters mentioned are: Pappachi, an Indian government official; his son Chacko, who was educated at Oxford University where he met his now ex-wife Margaret; Chacko's sister Ammu; Rahel and Estha, Ammu's young twin daughter and son.*

When he died, Pappachi left trunks full of expensive suits and a cholocate tin full of cuff-links that Chacko distributed among the taxi drivers in Kottayam. They were separated and made into rings and pendants for unmarried daughters' dowries.

When the twins asked what cuff-links were for – "To link cuffs together," Ammu told them – they were thrilled by this morsel of logic in what had so far seemed an illogical language. *Cuff+link = Cuff-link*. This, to them, rivalled the precision and logic of mathematics. *Cuff-links* gave them an inordinate (if exaggerated) satisfaction, and a real affection for the English language.

Ammu said that Pappachi was an incurable British CCP, which was short for *chhi-chhi poach* and in Hindi meant shit-wiper. Chacko said that the correct word for people like Pappachi was *Anglophile*. He made Rahel and Estha look up *Anglophile* in the *Reader's Digest Great Encyclopaedic Dictionary*. It said *Person well disposed to the English*. Then Estha and Rahel had to look up *disposed*. It said: (1) *Place suitably in particular order.* (2) *Bring mind into certain state.* (3) *Do what one will with, get off one's hands, stow away, demolish, finish, settle, consume (food), kill, sell.*

Chacko said that in Pappachi's case it meant (2) *Bring mind into certain state*. Which, Chacko said, meant that Pappachi's mind had been *brought into a state* which made him like the English.

Chacko told the twins that though he hated to admit it, they were all Anglophiles. They were a *family* of Anglophiles. Pointed in the wrong direction, trapped outside their own history, and unable to retrace their steps because their footprints had been swept away. He explained to them that history was like an old house at night. With all the lamps lit. And ancestors whispering inside.

"To understand history," Chacko said, "we have to go inside and listen to what they're saying. And look at the books and the pictures on the wall. And smell the smells."

Estha and Rahel had no doubt that the house Chacko meant was the house on the other side of the river, in the middle of the abandoned rubber estate where they had never been. Kari Saipu's house. The Black Sahib. The Englishman who had 'gone native'. Who spoke Malayalam and wore mundus. Ayemenem's own Kurtz. Ayemenem his private Heart of Darkness. He had shot himself through the head ten years ago when his young lover's parents had taken the boy away from him and sent him to school. After the suicide, the property had become the subject of extensive litigation between Kari Saipu's cook and his secretary. The house had lain empty for years. Very few people had seen it. But the twins could picture it.

The History House.

With cool stone floors and dim walls and billowing ship-shaped shadows. Plump, translucent lizards lived behind old pictures, and waxy, crumbling ancestors with tough toe-nails and breath that smelled of yellow maps gossiped in sibilant, papery whispers.

FACT FILE

Even after independence, British influence in India remained very strong, not least because the sons of wealthy families were often sent to Britain for their education. Nehru, Prime Minister between 1947 and 1964, who was educated at the top public school Harrow and Cambridge University before qualifying as a lawyer in London, was not only joking when he called himself "the last Englishman to rule India".

---

[1] **trunk** large box for transporting clothes
[2] **cuff-link** *Manschettenknopf*
[2] **Kottayam** city in Kerala
[4] **dowry** objects brought by a bride to her husband
[6] **morsel** very small piece
[8] **inordinate** unusually large
[9] **affection** liking
[16] **to stow** to store
[16] **to settle** *here:* to give to sb
[23] **to retrace** to go back over
[25] **ancestor** person one is descended from
[30] **estate** *here:* area of land where crop is cultivated
[32] **mundu** cloth worn around lower part of the body
[32] **Ayemenem** town, part of Kottayam
[33] **Kurtz** character in the 1902 story 'Heart of Darkness' by Joseph Conrad
[36] **litigation** legal disagreement
[40] **dim** not bright
[40] **billowing** swelling
[41] **plump** rather fat
[41] **lizard** *Eidechse*
[41] **crumbling** falling to pieces
[42] **to gossip** to pass on (often untrue) news about people
[43] **sibilant** with a hissing sound

38

East meets West

"But we can't go in," Chacko explained, "because we've been locked out. And when we look in through the windows, all we see are shadows. And when we try to listen, all we hear is a whispering. And we cannot understand the whispering, because our minds have been invaded by a war. A war that we have won and lost. The very worst sort of war. A war that captures dreams and re-dreams them. A war that has made us adore our conquerors and despise ourselves."

"*Marry* our conquerors, is more like it," Ammu said drily, referring to Margaret Kochamma. Chacko ignored her. He made the twins look up *Despise*. It said: *To look down upon; to view with contempt; to scorn or disdain.*

Chacko said that in the context of the war he was talking about – the War of Dreams – *Despise* meant all those things.

"We're Prisoners of War," Chacko said. "Our dreams have been doctored. We belong nowhere. We sail unanchored on troubled seas. We may never be allowed ashore. Our sorrows will never be sad enough. Our joys never happy enough. Our dreams never big enough. Our lives never important enough. To matter."

Then, to give Estha and Rahel a sense of historical perspective (though perspective was something which, in the weeks to follow, Chacko himself would sorely lack), he told them about the Earth Woman. He made them imagine that the earth – four thousand six hundred million years old – was a forty-six-year-old woman – as old, say, as Aleyamma Teacher, who gave them Malayalam lessons. It had taken the whole of the Earth Woman's life for the earth to become what it was. For the oceans to part. For the mountains to rise. The Earth Woman was eleven years old, Chacko said, when the first single-celled organisms appeared. The first animals, creatures like worms and jellyfish, appeared only when she was forty. She was over forty-five – just eight months ago – when dinosaurs roamed the earth.

"The whole of human civilization as we know it," Chacko told the twins, "began only *two hours* ago in the Earth Woman's life. As long as it takes us to drive from Ayemenem to Cochin."

It was an awe-inspiring and humbling thought, Chacko said (*Humbling* was a nice word, Rahel thought. *Humbling along without a care in the world*), that the whole of contemporary history, the World Wars, the War of Dreams, the Man on the Moon, science, literature, philosophy, the pursuit of knowledge – was no more than a blink of the Earth Woman's eye.

"And we, my dears, everything we are and ever will be – are just a twinkle in her eye," Chacko said grandly, lying on his bed, staring at the ceiling.

When he was in this sort of mood, Chacko used his Reading Aloud voice. His room had a church-feeling. He didn't care whether anyone was listening to him or not. And if they were, he didn't care whether or not they had understood what he was saying. Ammu called them his Oxford Moods.

From: Arundhati Roy, *The God of Small Things*, 1997

VIP FILE

Arundhati Roy
born 1961; spent childhood in Kerala; started career by writing screenplays for television and cinema; 1997 won Booker Prize for first novel 'The God of Small Things'; also campaigns for social causes, both in India and globally; lives in New Delhi

⁵²**contempt** feeling that sb or sth is worthless
⁵²**to scorn** to refuse to accept
⁵²**to disdain** to consider not good enough
⁵⁷**ashore** on dry land
⁵⁷**sorrow** sadness
⁶¹**sorely** to a high degree
⁶⁷**jellyfish** *Qualle*
⁶⁹**to roam** to move around with no definite aim
⁷²**Cochin** port in Kerala
⁷³**awe-inspiring** causing one to feel wonder and respect
⁷³**humbling** causing one to feel unimportant
⁷⁶**pursuit** *here:* seeking
⁷⁸**twinkle** small light changing constantly in intensity
⁷⁹**grandly** *here:* sounding important

1 Examine how Chacko is characterised. How do references to other members of the family help to give emphasis to the way in which he is portrayed?

2 a) Explain Chacko's view of the effect of being a family of Anglophiles and what this means to their identity.
b) Comment on Chacko's comparing history to an old house at night. Come up with other similes you could use to describe history.

WORD BANK
to feel superior • pedantic • to hold forth on a subject • oratory style • high-flown language/ideas • to talk over sb's head

4 East meets West

1 *Thinking about India's ethnic and religious diversity and also the huge number of languages spoken (22 of which have official status today), what problems would you expect concerning government and administration? What solutions can you think of?*

The world as India

English has become the common language that unifies linguistic disparities. India has sixteen "official languages"² (actually, many more vernacular² languages are spoken), and there is no way that India, given its present composition and diversity, which includes 180 million Muslims, is ever going to agree to, say, the principal language, Hindi, becoming the national language. The language that could be a national language would precisely not be a native one but the language of the conqueror, of the colonial era. Just because it is alien, foreign, it can become the unifying language of a permanently diverse people: the only language that all Indians might have in common not only is, has to be, English.

The computer has only reinforced the pre-eminence of English in our global India. Surely some of the most interesting linguistic phenomena of our era are the disappearance of many lesser languages – that is, languages spoken by very small, isolated, impoverished peoples – and the unique success of English, which now has a status unlike any other language used on the planet. English is now advancing in every part of the world, through the dominance of English-speaking media – which means media in which English is spoken with an American accent – and the need for business people and scientists to communicate in a common language. […]

At the other extreme, a more recent example of what is involved in attaining perfect mastery in a second language – which happens to be English – gives us a perfect scenario of inauthenticity. I am thinking about one flourishing enterprise in the multi-billion software industry now so important to the Indian economy. These are the call centers, employing many thousands of young women and men who give technical help to take reservations made by dialing 1-800 (that is, toll-free numbers all over the United States). The young people, all of whom already speak English, who compete successfully for these coveted²⁶ jobs in the call centers, and have completed the arduous²⁷ course designed to erase all traces of their Indian accent in English (many fail), are being paid what is a munificent²⁸ salary for office work in India, though of course far less than what IBM, American Express, GE, Delta Airlines, and chains of hotels and restaurants would have to pay to Americans to do the job – reason enough for more and more such tasks to be "outsourced". It also seems to be the case that the Indians perform the tasks better, with fewer errors, which is not surprising, since virtually all of them have college degrees.

VIP FILE

Susan Sontag, 1933–2004, was a prize-winning American writer and political activist, best known for her essays, in which she expressed a critical view of western civilisation. Apart from writing short stories, novels, essays, reviews and films, which she directed herself, she also directed plays in the USA and Europe.

---

²sixteen official languages by now 22 have been acknowledged
²vernacular local language of a particular region
²⁶coveted *(fml)* much desired
²⁷arduous involving a lot of effort
²⁸munificent *(fml)* large and generous

From large floors of office buildings in Bangalore or Bombay or New Delhi, call after call is answered by young Indians seated in rows of small booths ("Hi, this is Nancy. How may I help you?"), each equipped with a computer that allows them to summon with a few clicks the relevant information to make a reservation, maps to give information about the best highway route, weather forecasts, and so forth. Nancy, or Mary Lou, Betty, Sally Jane, Megan, Bill, Jim, Wally, Frank – these cheerful voices had first to be trained for months, by instructors and by tapes, to acquire a pleasant middle-American (not educated American) accent, and to learn basic American slang, informal idioms (including regional ones), and elementary mass-culture references (TV personalities and the plots and protagonists of the main sitcoms, the latest blockbuster in the multiplex, fresh baseball and basketball scores, and such), so that if the exchange with the United States becomes prolonged, they will not falter with the small talk and will have the means to continue to pass for Americans.

To pull this off, they have to be plausibly American to themselves. They have been assigned American names and little biographies of their American identities: place and date of birth, parents' occupation, number of siblings, religious denomination (almost always Protestant), high school, favourite sport, favourite kind of music, marital status, and the like. If asked where they are, they have a reply. For example, if the client is calling from Savannah, Georgia, to make a reservation in a hotel in Macon, Georgia, and is asking directions for the quickest way to drive from Savannah to Macon, the operator might say she or he is in Atlanta. Letting on that they are in Bangalore, India, would get pretend-Nancy or pretend-Bill instantly fired. (All the calls are routinely, and undetectably, monitored by supervisors.) And of course virtually none of these young people has ever left home. Would "Nancy" or "Bill" prefer to be a real Nancy and a real Bill? Almost all say – there have been interviews – that they would. Would they want to come to America, where it would be normal to speak English all the time with an American accent? Of course they would.

From: Susan Sontag, "The World as India", in: *At the Same Time,* 2007

R&D Research and development
[38]**to summon** *here: aufrufen*
[47]**to falter** to become weak or unsure
[50]**to be assigned sth** to be given sth
[51]**siblings** *(fml)* brothers and sisters
[53]**marital status** *(fml) Familienstand*

2 Explain the development and role of English as a lingua franca in India and discuss positive and negative effects.

3 Comment on what Sontag reports about call centres and their employees. Would you mind assuming a different identity to do a job? Why (not)?

4 [🎬] Look at the following tasks before you watch the video, take notes while watching and do the tasks afterwards.
  1. Describe the visual contrast presented at the beginning of the clip. Say why the shopping mall is or is not as you would have expected.
  2. Point out the problems that are referred to in the context of the reform and development of India's economy.
  3. Explain the perspective of international business leaders and the implications of this for India.
  4. Sum up and comment on the presenter's final thoughts on the situation.

5 [👥] *After viewing:* Do a role play in the form of a discussion on 'Which way should India go?' between an Indian politician, an Indian business leader, an American industrialist and an anti-globalisation activist. Prepare for your roles by thinking and making notes about your point of view.

WORD BANK
International business
outsourcing • skilled workforce • multinational companies • global markets • competition • cost-minimisation • tech support • service sector • cubicle • digitalisation • telecommunication • lingua franca • foreign investment • economic policies • to undertake reforms • to set priorities • to meet special needs • (not) to be dictated to by

4 East meets West

Paul Theroux, born in 1941 in Massachusetts, has lived in Africa, Singapore, England and Hawaii. As a travel writer and novelist he is well-known for his lively descriptions of life in foreign countries.

[5 ⦿] The Gateway of India

On these stifling days in Mumbai, when a meeting dragged on, Dwight hitched himself in his chair and looked at the spot where his life had changed. From the height of the boardroom on the top floor of Jeejeebhoy Towers, where Mahatma Gandhi crossed Church Gate, he could see down the long table and out the window, to marvel at it and to reflect on how far he'd come. He loved the Gateway of India for its three portals, open to the sea on one side, land on the other. He regarded it as something personal, a monumental souvenir, an imperial archway, attracting a crowd – the ice cream sellers, the nut vendors, the balloon hawkers, the beggars, and the girls looking for men.

Eight Indians sat at the gleaming conference table, four on either side, and he, Dwight Huntsinger, visiting American, lawyer and moneyman, was at the head of it.

"You are a necessary devil," M.V. Desai, the industrialist, had joked. Objecting to the preening boldness of the man, Dwight smiled, saying, "You bet your sweet ass I am."

The man was worth millions. Everyone at the table winced, but Dwight's remark was calculated: they would never forget it.

An assortment of roof tiles were scattered on the table – samples, to be manufactured somewhere in Maharashtra. Also a bottle of water and a glass with a paper cap at each place, a yellow pad, pencils, dishes of – what? – some sort of food, hard salty peas, yellow potato lumps, spicy garbanzos, something that looked like wood shavings, something else like twigs, bundles of cheese straws.

"It's all nuts and cheese balls at this table," Dwight had said the first day, another way of responding to M.V. Desai, another calculation. They had stared at him as though they'd just heard bad news. None of the food looked edible. Although it was his second trip to India, he had not so far touched any Indian food. He did not think of it as food; all of it looked lethal.

Get me out of here had been his constant thought. India had been an ordeal for him, but he had chosen it in a willful way, knowing it was reckless. It was deliberate. Recently divorced, he had said to his ex-wife in their last phone call, "Maureen, listen carefully. I'm going to India," as if he were jumping off a bridge. It was the day he received her engagement ring back – no note, just a diamond ring, sent by FedEx to his office – and he was hoping she'd feel bad. But as though to spite him, she said, "It'll probably change your life," and he thought, Bitch!

That was the first trip, a week of Indian hell – a secular hallucinatory underworld of actual grinning demons and foul unbreathable air. He had dreaded it, and it had exceeded even his fearful expectations – dirtier, smellier,

---

[1] **stifling** making you feel as if you cannot breathe properly
[5] **to marvel at sth** to be filled with surprise and admiration about sth
[14] **preening** self-satisfied
[21] **garbanzo** *Kichererbse*
[27] **lethal** deadly
[28] **ordeal** a difficult and extremely unpleasant experience
[34] **to spite sb** to do sth nasty deliberately to annoy sb
[34] **bitch** *(rude)* a woman who behaves in a nasty way

42

more chaotic and unforgiving than anywhere he'd ever been. "Hideous" did not describe it; there were no words for it. It was like an experience of grief, leaving you mute and small.

The worst of it was that the Indians never ceased to praise it, gloating over it, saying how much they loved it. But it was a horror, and here was his discovery: the horror didn't stop; it went on repeating; he turned a corner and went down a new street and his senses were assaulted again, the sidewalks like freak shows.

"You seem a good deal disappointed," Mr. Shah said. Shah, the point man, was his guide in everything.

"Not disappointed," Dwight said. "I'm disgusted. I'm frightened. I am appalled. Don't you see I want to go home?" In this world of anguish he felt physically hurt by what he saw. But it continued for the days he was there and did not stop until he had gotten back on the plane and left the smell of failure, of futility, of death and disease, returning to Boston with another discovery: in all that misery, there was money. [...]

Extreme measures. He brought a supply of tuna fish, the small cans with pop-off lids, and crackers, and Gatorade. It was like a prison diet, but it would be bearable and appropriate for his seven days of captivity in Mumbai. These he would spend in the best room at the best hotel: the Elephanta Suite at the Taj Mahal Hotel, just across the Gateway.

Yet he was ashamed of himself, standing in his hotel bathroom of polished marble and gilt fittings, leaning over the sink, eating tuna fish out of a can with a plastic fork. Three days of that, three days of Shah's saying, "You must see Crawford Market and Chor Bazaar. Perhaps Elephanta Caves, perhaps side trip to Agra to see Taj? What you want to see?"

"The Gateway of India."

"Very nice. Three portal arches. Tripulia of Gujarati design. Not old, put up by British in 1927. But …" Shah widened his mouth grinning in confusion.

"What?"

"You can see it from here."

"That's what I like about it."

India was a foreign country where he'd been assigned to find outsourcing deals, not a place to enjoy but one to endure, like going down a dark hole to find jewels. He worked in the boardroom, wrangling with manufacturers; he sat in his suite and watched CNN. His grimmest pleasure was looking through the classifieds of the Hindustan Times, the pages headed "Matrimonials", and he smiled in disbelief at the willingness in the details, the eagerness of the girls desperate to be brides, the boys to be grooms. His disillusionment with marriage was compounded by his misery in India. He suffered, and the firm was grateful, for India proved to be outsourcing heaven.

From: Paul Theroux, "The Gateway of India", in: *The Elephanta Suite*, 2007

[38] **hideous** extremely unpleasant or ugly
[41] **to cease** to stop
[41] **to gloat** *(disapproving)* to show great pleasure, often in an arrogant way
[48] **anguish** great pain and suffering
[51] **futility** total lack of purpose
[54] **lid** top of a container that can be opened
[54] **Gatorade** a kind of soft drink
[59] **marble** *Marmor*
[59] **gilt fittings** taps covered with gold
[69] **to assign sb** to delegate
[73] **classifieds** small ads *(BE)*
[73] **matrimonials** marriage advertisements

WORD BANK

word field • sensuality • imagery • pun • exaggeration • symbol • to stand for • to reflect • comparison • metaphor • contrast • connotation • point of view • hierarchy • body language • thoughts and feelings • character • relationships • repulsive • to be disgusted • to be fascinated • to resist • to demonstrate power/superiority • to be frustrated • intolerant • benevolent • to take pride in sth • to feel attracted by sth • to feel attached to sb/sth

1 a) *Characterise Dwight Huntsinger and explain what business he has in India.*
   b) *Compare his attitude towards India with the quotations on pages 4/5 and point out the stylistic devices used to portray this attitude. Comment on the role of food in the text.*

2 a) *Examine and explain the way Shah and Huntsinger deal with each other.*
   b) *Write another dialogue between them.*

3 [🖥] *Find out about the Taj Mahal in Agra and the Elephanta Caves near Mumbai. Write a short article about these two places for a travel guide.*

4 East meets West

[🖥 Online-Link: **601006-0018**]

1 *Before reading:* Think about the clothes you are wearing right now. What do you know about where they were made and who made them?

Fashion's dirty secret

¹**boho** *(infml)* Bohemian
²**to be credited with** to be acknowledged for sth
²**retro** copying a style from the recent past
²**high street** area with shops
⁶**to be swamped with** to have too much of sth
⁷**embroidery** *Stickerei*
¹⁴**to eradicate** to put an end to
¹⁸**cramped** having too little space
²¹**catwalk** platform for models in fashion shows
²¹**sewer** channel for carrying away water and waste
²⁸**to stitch** to sew
²⁹**to glisten** to shine
²⁹**bead** small piece of glass or stone used in jewellery or to decorate clothes
²⁹**taut** fully stretched
³⁰**frame** structure for holding or supporting sth
³²**zari** Indian embroidery

The fashion world called it "boho chic". Sienna Miller, the model and actress, was credited with creating the retro hippie look that swept Britain's high streets last spring, but according to human rights campaigners many of the clothes were made in India by children as young as seven.

Exporters in Delhi said last week that sales had increased by more than 60 % as the fashion caught on. Swamped with orders, many had to subcontract embroidery to small workshops and middle-men. [...]

Arun Bhutani, whose export company supplies Topshop and other leading high street names, said he had had so many orders from Britain and the United States for embroidery that he subcontracted out much of the work and had no idea whether child labour was used. "We don't allow child labour in the factory, but there's no guarantee that it was not used. It's not possible for everybody to check everything," he admitted.

The campaigners say this is what the fashion industry must do to eradicate child labour. They are calling on designers and high street chains to guarantee that children have not made any part of their clothes, bags and shoes. [...]

The international fashion industry's dirty secret is hidden in hundreds of cramped, dusty workshops on the outskirts of Delhi where an estimated 100,000 children work up to 14 hours a day. The largely Muslim slums in Delhi's Selampur and Kalakar suburbs could not be more remote from the glamour of the catwalk. In narrow lanes with open sewers, there are hundreds of one-room workshops, in each of which up to 15 children are forced to work long days for less than 3p an hour. The workshops are filled with children from some of India's poorest states, including Bihar and Jharkhand.

In one of 10 workshops visited by The Sunday Times sat Fayaz, who appeared to be no older than eight, and Darinder, who claimed to be 15, but looked 12. The two boys had been taken out of school in Bihar and brought to Delhi by their families. They were sitting back-to-back on a thin, rough carpet, each stitching tiny, glistening beads into patterns on pink chiffons stretched taut on wooden frames. They and 11 other children worked from 9am to 9pm, with an hour's lunch break, they said. They have one day off a week. They sleep on the floor beneath the zari frames.

Fayaz has an angelic face but his expression is fearful. He checks the boss is not listening before saying he does not know how old he is. "I earn 300 rupees [£3.50] a week. I miss my friends," he said. "I went to school and I miss it." Darinder was handed over to the workshop two years ago after his mother died, leaving his father, a farmer, to raise him and his three brothers and sisters. "I earn 2,000 rupees a month. One thousand rupees goes in my pocket, the other 1,000 is sent home. I want to go home," he said. [...]

Last week the Indian government banned children from working as domestic servants or in hotels, cafes and roadside snack stands. The law on other sectors remains unclear.

Dean Nelson, *The Sunday Times*, October 15, 2006

East meets West

2 *Describe* in what sense child labour in India is a 'secret'. Point out what the problem is in guaranteeing that child labour is not used in the fashion industry.

3 *Discuss:* Child labour is preferable to starvation for that child's family.

4 *Write a letter to* The Sunday Times *giving your reaction to the article and outlining your ideas about who bears responsibility for child labour and what can be done to try and eradicate it.*

5 *Mediation:* Bollywood has helped to popularise Indian style and fashion in the west. Summarise the information in this text for an American friend.

> **WORD BANK**
> **Letter to the editor**
> Sir, … • I wish to respond to … • … makes me feel … • I cannot accept the excuse that … • Everyone in the chain including the consumer … • … must be prepared to …

Träume in Pink, Gold, Orange

Ob Filme, Mode oder Musik – Bollywood-Fieber in Deutschland. Jetzt bringen zwei große Bühnenshows noch mehr knallbunte Illusionen aus Indien.

Die weiße Mauer ist unüberwindbar, das Firmenschild ‚Yash Raj Studio' diskret, die Sicherheitskontrolle ausdauernd. Wenn man schließlich das blickdichte Tor zu Indiens größtem Filmstudio mitten im regenzeittrüben Mumbai (Bombay) passiert, denkt man unwillkürlich: Wie viele der Menschen, die du auf dem Weg hierher beobachtet hast, würden dich jetzt beneiden?

Die Fahrer der giftgrün und gelb lackierten Motorrikschas, die sich durch schlammbraune Straßenströme pflügen. Die Kioskverkäufer, die Zeitungen und Vadapav-Snacks unter Plastikplanen vor den Güssen schützen. Die schwer schuftenden Wäscher in den steinernen Becken des Dhobi Ghat, nass von unten und oben. Die Straßenjungs, die an der Ampel eine Menschenpyramide bauen, um den Wartenden ein paar Münzen abzutrotzen. Sie alle würden viel geben für einen Besuch in der Traumfabrik Bollywood, wo ihre Superstars ein- und ausgehen. Jene wie Götter verehrten Helden und Diven, die mit herzzerreißenden Liebesdramen, großen Tanzszenen und Liedern drei Stunden Ablenkung schenken vom harten Leben in der 16-Millionen-Metropole.

Der Alltag der Traumfabrik sieht erst mal nüchterner aus: Schneider an uralten Nähmaschinen passen Glitzerkostüme wie am Fließband an. Gelangweilt stehen muskulöse Jungs herum, bildschöne Mädchen in Jeans schlagen die Zeit in der Raucherecke tot. Filme drehen heißt auch in Bollywood vor allem: warten. Doch jetzt rauscht, unspektakulär in Jeans und weiß-türkis geblümter Bluse, leibhaftige Prominenz in den Proberaum von Bollywood – The Show. Auftritt Vaibhavi Merchant. Ihre Biografie liefert den Handlungsrahmen für das Bühnenspektakel, das hier einstudiert, genauer: zwischen Australien- und Europatournee aufgefrischt wird. Die preisgekrönte Choreografin Merchant hat bei Kino-Kassenschlagern wie Hum Dil de Chuke Sanaam oder Lagaan mitgewirkt und zuletzt beim Liebesdrama Fanaa, das in Kaschmir spielt und – welch ein Verstoß gegen die Bollywood-Regeln! – unhappy endet. Allein im Jahr 2004 kamen 16 Filme heraus, bei denen Merchants Name im Abspann lief.

Und Choreografie ist mehr als Beiwerk im Hindifilm! Die ausufernden Tanznummern sind ein unverzichtbares Element des typischen ‚Massala-Movie', das, zusammengeschüttelt wie die scharfe Gewürzmischung, hemmungslos alles zugleich ist: Liebesschnulze und Komödie, Gangsterfilm und Moritat, Videoclip und Meditation. Die Tanzeinlagen können das alles verbinden, aber auch ihre eigenen Geschichten erzählen, und manchmal tun sie nicht mal das. Sie sind Massala im Massala: eine Melange aus Schritten und Gesten, die indische Klassik, regionale Volkstänze, Elemente aus HipHop und Jazztanz, Michael-Jackson-Style und Ginger-Rogers-Romantik, Ringelreihen und Freistil verschmelzen. Rund 200 Filme kommen jedes Jahr aus Mumbai; darüber hinaus werden in Tamil Nadu, Kerala und anderen Bundesstaaten etwa 600 weitere Filme in lokalen Sprachen und auch Autorenfilme gedreht.

Christiane Grefe, *Die Zeit*, 21. September 2006

4 East meets West

1 What do you think it is like for young people brought up in traditional Indian society to emigrate to the US?

2 Listen, and talk about what is special about the Indian accent of the speaker.

[6 ⊙] Jasmine

The novel Jasmine *(1989) is about a young Hindu woman who leaves India to seek a new life in the United States. This extract describes Jasmine's first meeting with the Hayes family, to whom she is introduced by a mutual friend called Kate.*

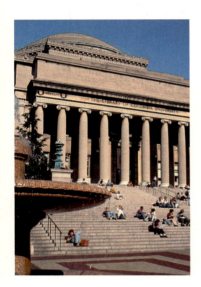

I became an American in an apartment on Claremont Avenue across the street from a Barnard College dormitory. I lived with Taylor and Wylie Hayes for nearly two years. Duff was my child; Taylor and Wylie were my parents, my teachers, my family.

I entered their life on a perfect spring Sunday. Kate and I left Sam in his corner of the loft, baking on a rock pile underneath a sunlamp, in the middle of a child's plastic wading pool, and took a bus all the way up Broadway to 116th Street, at the gates of Columbia University. The sky had a special penetrating blueness, the temperature and humidity made it seem we were breathing through our skin. We went down the hill toward the river, then turned in at the first building. The street was Claremont Avenue and all the apartments belonged to Columbia teachers, true professorjis. I expected the air itself to crackle with so much intelligence.

Wylie and Taylor and their little girl, Duff, met us with tea and biscuits. They were in their early thirties, and dressed like students in T-shirts and cords. Taylor had teeth as crooked as mine – the first crooked teeth I'd seen in America – with a gap between his front teeth wide enough to hold a matchstick. He had a blondish beard. Wylie was tall and blond, thin as a schoolgirl, with a pair of dark glasses pushed high in her hair, and a pair of regular glasses resting on her chest, held by a chain around her neck. Duff immediately asked my name and where I was from. "You know where India is, darling. Remember, we found it on the map." She took out a piece of paper and tried to spell my name. I had never seen a small child, especially a girl, who could immediately relate to adults, call them by their first names, and break into their conversations.

She asked Kate, "Where's my Sammy?" Kate reminded her that Sam and city buses were not on good terms. The one time she'd taken him on a bus, wrapped like a baby but for his breathing holes, the crested tail had popped from the blanket, the tongue had darted, and a man sitting next to them had drawn a knife in self-defense. Thereafter she left him at home in what Duff called Sammy's Ocean.

I asked what kind of pets the Hayeses had. Fortunately, the university permitted nothing as exotic as iguanas and snakes, only the usual dogs, cats, rabbits, hamsters, gerbils, – none of which Duff could tolerate because of allergies.

"We might have to move if Duff wants an ostrich or something," said Taylor. Duff giggled. Kate prompted me to smile.

Silence fell. I nibbled a biscuit.

"I hope $95 a week is satisfactory," said Wylie. "I've checked around, and that's a little low, but there really shouldn't be any other expenses –"

I had not imagined money, dollars, for sleeping with a child. "That is very good," I said.

²**dormitory** building in which students live
⁵**Sam** name of a pet iguana
⁶**loft** *here:* open-style flat on the top floor of a building
⁹**humidity** amount of water in the atmosphere
¹²**-ji** *(Hindi)* used with names and titles to show respect
¹²**to crackle** to make the sound of sparks
¹⁵**cords** corduroy trousers
¹⁶**crooked** not straight
¹⁹**chest** front of upper body
²⁶**to be on good terms** to have a friendly relationship
²⁷**crested** (of animals) having a comb of fur or skin on the head
³³**gerbil** *Wüstenrennmaus*
³⁵**ostrich** *Strauß*
³⁶**to prompt** to give a signal to sb to do or say sth

"I'm not going to ask you for references, Jasmine," she went on. "Kate's already told us something about you. […] You will be part of the family. Families don't go around requiring references."

45 "Anyway, Sam already approved you," said Taylor. "Being cold-blooded, he doesn't warm to many people. In fact, he has a godlike perspective on the whole mammal class."

He smiled his crooked-toothed smile, and I began to fall in love. I mean, I fell in love with what he represented to me, a professor who served biscuits to a
50 servant, smiled at her, and admitted her to the broad democracy of his joking, even when she didn't understand it. It seemed entirely American. I was curious about his life, not repulsed. I wanted to know the way such a man lives in this country. I wanted to watch, be a part of it. He seemed wondrously extravagant, that Sunday morning.

55 I didn't have the slightest understanding of anything they said, and they didn't bother explaining. I liked that, the assumption behind it.
Wylie said that Duff was adopted.
"Low sperm count," she explained.
I blushed, but neither Wylie nor Taylor noticed.
60 "Hockey injury," Taylor protested.

They planned to tell Duff everything when she was old enough. They'd even let her meet her natural mother, currently a sophomore at Iowa State University. Their lawyer had placed ads in small-town Iowa and Nebraska and Kansas newspapers, asking pregnant unwed girls to contact him. Wylie and Taylor were
65 paying for the girl's education. I remember thinking an Iowa newspaper must be in a language called Iowan like a Punjabi or a Spanish newspaper. I liked the mystery. Duff looked perfectly American.

"We could have gotten a child out of Paraguay," Taylor explained. "The Needhams on the sixth floor got their baby from Paraguay. They had to go down
70 and hang around for six weeks in this nothing village full of Nazi war criminals, and the way they described the whole thing, it sounded awful, sort of like a direct sale."

I could not imagine a non-genetic child. A child that was not my own, or my husband's, struck me as a monstrous idea. Adoption was as foreign to me as the
75 idea of widow remarriage.

I looked out into the dorm windows across Claremont Avenue. The windows were long, bright, shadeless rectangles of light. No window shades, no secrets. Barnard women were studying cross-legged on narrow beds, changing T-shirts, clowning with Walkmans clamped to their heads. They wore nothing under their
80 shirts and sweaters. Men were in their room. Even on the first morning I saw naked bodies combing their hair in front of dresser mirrors. Truly there was no concept of shame in this society.

From: Bharati Mukherjee, *Jasmine*, 1989

VIP FILE

Bharati Mukherjee, born 1940 in Calcutta; went to the US to study creative writing in 1961; lived in Canada 1968–1980 before returning to the US, is now a professor at University of Berkeley, California. Her novels mainly deal with Asian immigrants in North America.

47 mammal *Säugetier*
50 to admit to to allow to enter
52 to be repulsed opposite of to be attracted
59 to blush to become red in the face with embarrassment
62 sophomore *(AE)* second-year student
64 unwed not married
77 shadeless without blinds
77 rectangle *Rechteck*
79 clamped fixed
81 dresser piece of furniture with drawers and a mirror on the top

3 a) *Point out why Jasmine is taken to meet the Hayes family.*
b) *Pick out details that show how Jasmine's reaction to what she sees and hears is influenced by her traditional Indian background.*
c) *Interpret the first sentence of the extract.*

4 *Analyse the narrative techniques used by the author and the effect they achieve. Think in particular about the narrative perspective, the use of description and comments, and the overall style of the language.*

4 East meets West

1 The Mistress of Spices *(1997) is a novel about Tilo, an Indian immigrant who runs a spice shop in Oakland, California. What no one knows is that before Tilo left for America she went to a secret island where she was trained by the Old One to use the magical power of spices. While you read the following extract, make a list of the spices mentioned, noting down any information given about them.*

[7◉] The Mistress of Spices

Let me tell you about chillies.

The dry chilli, *lanka*, is the most potent of spices. In its blister-red skin, the most beautiful. Its other name is danger.

The chilli sings in the voice of a hawk circling sun-bleached hills where nothing grows. *I* lanka *was born of Agni, god of fire. I dripped from his fingertips to bring taste to this bland earth.*

Lanka, I think I am most in love with you.

The chilli grows in the very centre of the island, in the core of a sleeping volcano. Until we reach the third level of apprenticeship, we are not allowed to approach it.

Chilli, spice of red Thursday, which is the day of reckoning. Day which invites us to pick up the sack of our existence and shake it inside out. Day of suicide, day of murder.

Lanka, lanka. Sometimes I roll your name over my tongue. Taste the enticing sting of it.

So many times the Old One has warned us against your powers.

"Daughters, use it only as the last remedy. It is easy to start a flame. But to put it out?"

That is why I hold on, *lanka*, whose name the ten-headed Ravana took for his enchanted kingdom. City of a million jewels turned at the last to ash. Though more than once I have been tempted.

As when Jagjit comes to the store.

In the inner room of the store, on the topmost shelf, sits a sealed jar filled with red fingers of light. One day I will open it and the chillies will flicker to the ground. And blaze.

Lanka, fire-child, cleanser of evil. For when there is no other way.

Jagjit comes to the store with his mother. Stands partly behind her, his fingers touching her *dupatta* although he is ten and a half already and tall as wild bamboo.

"Oi Jaggi don't hang on me like a girl, go get me a packet of *sabu papads*."

Jagjit with his thin, frightened wrists who has trouble in school because he knows only Punjabi still. Jagjit whom the teacher has put in the last row next to the drooling boy with milk-blue eyes. Jagjit who has learned his first English word. Idiot. Idiot. Idiot.

I walk to the back where he stares in confusion at the shelves of *papads*, the packets stamped with hieroglyphs of Hindi and English.

I hand him the *sabu papads*. I tell him, "They're the bumpy white ones, see. Next time you'll know."

Shy-eyed Jagjit in your green turban that the kids at school make fun of, do you know your name means world-conqueror?

But already his mother is shouting, "What's taking you so long, Jaggi, can't find the *papads*, are you blind, the hairs on my head will go white waiting waiting by the time you get back."

FACT FILE
The Ramayana, the great Hindu epic, tells how the evil Ravana, ruler of the island kingdom of Lanka, carries off the beautiful Sita, wife to Rama. In the fight by Rama to rescue her, Lanka is burnt and reduced to ash.

mistress woman in position of control or authority
[4]**hawk** *Habicht*
[5]**to drip** to fall in small amounts
[6]**bland** *(of food)* lacking taste
[8]**core** central part of sth
[9]**apprenticeship** training
[11]**reckoning** judging
[14]**to entice** to attract
[15]**sting** pain
[17]**remedy** cure
[19]**to hold on** *here:* to wait
[20]**enchanted** under the power of magic
[21]**to tempt** to try to persuade sb to do sth wrong
[23]**sealed** closed so that air cannot get in
[23]**jar** glass or pot used to store food
[24]**to flicker** *here:* to make small, quick movements
[25]**to blaze** to burn fiercely
[28]**dupatta** *(Hindi)* cloth used to cover head
[30]**sabu** *(Gujarati)* tapioca
[30]**papad** *(Tamil)* circular piece of spiced bread
[31]**wrist** *Handgelenk*
[33]**to drool** *sabbern*
[37]**bumpy** not flat

East meets West

In the playground they try to pull it off his head, green turban the colour of a
parrot's breast. They dangle the cloth from their fingertips and laugh at his long,
uncut hair. And push him down.

Asshole, his second English word. And his knees bleeding from the gravel.

Jagjit who bites down on his lip so the cry will not out. Who picks up his
muddy turban and ties it on slowly and goes inside.

"Jaggi, how come you're always dirtying your school clothes, here is a button
gone and look at this big tear on your shirt, you *badmash*, you think I'm made of
money."

At night he lies with his eyes open, staring until the stars begin to flicker
like fireflies in his grandmother's *kheti* outside Jullunder. She is singing as she
gathers for dinner bunches of *saag* green as his turban. Punjabi words that
sound like rain.

Jagjit, do they come back when you at last must close your eyes because what
else can you do. The jeering voices, the spitting mouths, the hands. The hands
that pull your pants down in the playground, and the girls looking.

"*Chhodo mainu.*"

"Talk English sonofabitch. Speak up nigger wetback asshole."

"Jaggi what you meaning you don't want to go to school, what for your father
is killing himself working working at the factory, two slaps will make you go."

"*Chhodo.*"

At the checkstand I say, "Here's some *burfi* for you, no no madam, no cost
for children." I see him bite eager into the brown sweet flavoured with clove and
cardamom and cinnamon. He smiles a small smile to answer mine.

Crushed clove and cardamom, Jagjit, to make your breath fragrant.
Cardamom which I will scatter tonight on the wind for you. North wind
carrying them to open your teacher's unseeing. And also sweet pungent clove,
lavang, spice of compassion. So your mother of a sudden looking up from
the washboard, pushing tired hair from her face, "Jaggi *beta*, tell me what
happened," will hold you in her soapsud arms.

And here is cinnamon, hollow dark bone that I tuck unseen in your turban
just before you go. Cinnamon friend-maker, cinnamon *dalchini* warm-brown as
skin, to find you someone who will take you by the hand, who will run with you
and laugh with you and say See this is America, it's not so bad.

And for the others with the pebble-hard eyes, cinnamon destroyer of
enemies to give you strength, strength which grows in your legs and arms and
mostly mouth till one day you shout *no* loud enough to make them, shocked,
stop.

From: Chitra Banerjee Divakaruni, *The Mistress of Spices*, 1997

---

45 **to dangle** to let hang loosely
47 **gravel** very small stones used to cover the ground
50 **how come** how does/did it happen that …?
51 **badmash** *(Urdu)* violent troublemaker
54 **firefly** *Leuchtkäfer*
54 **kheti** *(Punjabi)* farm
54 **Jullunder** city in Punjab
55 **saag** *(Hindi)* Spinat
58 **to jeer** to laugh in a rude and insulting manner
60 **Chhodo mainu** *(Hindi/Punjabi)* Leave me alone!
61 **wetback** *(AE) (sl)* illegal immigrant
65 **checkstand** *(AE)* place in a store where one pays
65 **burfi** *(Hindi)* type of sweet
66 **clove** *(Gewürz)Nelke*
67 **cardamom** *Kardamom*
67 **cinnamon** *Zimt*
68 **to crush** to squeeze
68 **fragrant** sweet-smelling
69 **to scatter** to throw or spread in all directions
70 **pungent** strong-smelling
71 **lavang** *(Hindi)* clove
71 **compassion** feeling for the suffering of others
72 **beta** *(Punjabi)* son
73 **soapsud** bubble made from soap and water
75 **dalchini** *(Hindi)* cinnamon
78 **pebble** small stone

VIP FILE

Chitra Banerjee Divakaruni
was born in Calcutta in 1956; 1976 moved to the US; lives in California; writes poetry, short stories and novels; work features Indian-born women torn between cultures and values; *The Mistress of Spices* was made into a film in 2005

---

2 a) *Describe how the text portrays the experience of Indian immigrants in America.*
b) *Interpret the role of spices in the context of the local Indian community.*

3 *Comment on how the style of writing reflects the content of the text.*

4 *Compare and contrast* Jasmine *and* The Mistress of Spices. *How would you sum up the atmosphere created in the two extracts? Who or what is the main focus? To what extent do the Indian protagonists identify with their new home?*

Projects

PROJECT 1: A cultural trip to India

Regions to choose from:
- The Himalayan North
- Rajasthan
- Kolkata and Orissa
- Karnataka
- Kerala
- Tamil Nadu
- The Golden Triangle: Delhi – Agra – Jaipur

and the separate state of Bangladesh

Scenario: You work for a travel agency and your task is to develop and promote a two-week cultural trip to a particular region of the Indian subcontinent. The trip is to be a complete package, including not only travel and accommodation, but also a varied programme of activities and experiences designed to give an insight into the character, culture and history of the region. Having first researched and planned your holiday, you will then give a multimedia presentation to the public at a 'World Travel Fair'.

STEP 1 – Form groups to work on different regions
Decide which of the regions marked on the map you would like to work on and join up with other students who are also interested in that region. Each group should have a minimum of four people in order to deal with the amount of work that will be involved, and each group should concentrate on a different region, so it might be necessary for some students to compromise on their first choice. Don't worry if this happens to you. All the regions on the map have a lot to offer!

STEP 2 – Organise the work to be done
Look again at the scenario above and also at the **Useful phrases** box on the opposite page, and then brainstorm ideas about what information you need to research in order to develop a successful holiday. Also discuss how you want to present your trip and what kind of materials etc. this involves. List all the tasks to be done and divide the work up (you might want to work individually or in pairs). Also make a timetable for completion of the various stages of the project.

STEP 3 – Collect the information and material you are responsible for
Think of various sources you can use and then work methodically through these to ensure you do not miss anything that might be relevant or helpful.

STEP 4 – Plan the trip and then prepare the promotion

In another big group session, share and discuss all the information and material you have collected. Make a final decision about what you do or do not want to include in the trip and then develop an itinerary for the two weeks. Knowing the programme, you can now prepare to showcase your trip. Decide on the exact form and organisation of your presentation, produce the advertising material you want to use, and practise what you want to say. Use the strengths of different members of your team to the maximum advantage of the group.

STEP 5 – Act out the 'World Travel Fair' scenario
Each group gives its presentation in turn, with everyone else taking the role of potential customers. Anyone interested in booking the holiday can then ask questions, which the travel agents should be prepared to answer.

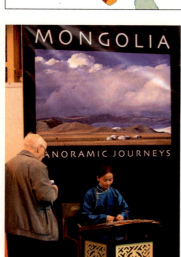

At a travel trade fair in Birmingham

Project 1

Useful phrases: Expressions for holiday bookings

Group tours:	Accommodation:
experienced/specialist tour operators complete/all-inclusive package typical group size: … carefully planned itinerary/programme escorted by a tour leader/local guide	5-star hotel with air-conditioning basic/luxurious level of comfort en-suite bathroom/shower centrally/conveniently located a range of guest facilities and services
Prices:	**Other information:**
inclusive of flights and transfers prices per person based on 2 adults sharing single-room occupancy for a supplement all entrance fees included a deposit of … is payable at the time of booking	visa required for all foreign nationals health advice and vaccinations currency/insurance/… services available

DELHI DISCOVERY ■ 3 DAYS/2 NIGHTS – PRIVATE TOUR
New Delhi colonial architecture ■ Old Delhi ■ Red Fort ■ Jama Masjid

Trailfinders' Delhi Discovery is an ideal way to get to know India's capital. Enjoy the contrast between New and Old Delhi with a tour that takes in the best the British left behind in New Delhi and the much more ancient temples and monuments from Indian history. Your tour of Delhi will include attractions such as the dramatic Red Fort, Jama Masjid – India's largest mosque and Chandni Chowk, once the richest street market in the world. The following day there is time to explore on your own, perhaps to bargain for handicrafts at the markets. The two evenings are free so that you can experience some of the fantastic dining available in the city. A perfect introduction to Delhi and India!
Inclusions: meet & greet • return private airport transfers • full day tour of Delhi's attractions • 2 nights' accommodation of your choice from our selection of hotels, please ask for details.
Departs: daily.
Price: from £178 per person.

Humayun's Tomb, Delhi

How to give a multimedia presentation

- Choose different media on the basis of how they can best contribute to your presentation, e.g. **music** to evoke a certain background atmosphere, large **photos** to create a visual impact, **video clips** to show an authentic scenario, **written material** to provide detailed information, **spoken commentary** to convey enthusiasm or give confidence etc.
- Structure your presentation so that you **capture your audience's interest immediately**, and then after that **give variety** to **maintain the level of interest**. While your presentation should be long enough to get across the points you want to make, it should also be short enough to hold attention throughout.
- Make a **plan** (e.g. notes, diagram, flow chart) showing the form and organisation of your presentation. This will also help you to **identify practical issues** that have to be dealt with. Do you need to make **prompt cards**? Have you got all the different kinds of **material** you want to present or hand out? What **technical equipment** do you need?
- **Rehearse** your presentation so that you are clear about **timings** and the **roles** and **tasks** for the various members of your team. Don't forget to **check the visibility, volume** etc. of your media. While keeping to your plan in general, also be prepared to be flexible to allow for **interaction** with your audience.

Project 2

PROJECT 2: A literary contest

The focus in this project is on four Indian authors who have won the prestigious Man Booker Prize: Salman Rushdie (1981), Arundhati Roy (1997), Kiran Desai (2006) and Aravind Adiga (2008). Your task is to hold a contest to decide which of the four is the best writer and therefore the overall literary champion.

STEP 1 – Create the framework for the contest
a) Decide on a name for the prize to be awarded at the end of the contest.
b) Form groups:
   - 4 smaller groups, each of which will support and present a different author.
   - 1 larger group to be the jury which will decide the winner.
c) Set a date for the contest so that you can plan your work accordingly.

STEP 2 – Do the preparatory work
a) **Each author group**
   Sharing the workload, carry out the following tasks:
   - Do background research on your author, including finding out about his or her major works and projects.
   - Acquire a copy of the novel that won the Booker Prize and get an overview of the whole book (plot, themes, structure, style etc.).
   - Find and make a literary analysis of specific passages which you feel show the author's talent and will therefore help you to champion him or her.
   - Plan, prepare and practise your presentation.
b) **Jury group**
   - Get together behind closed doors to discuss your ideas about what helps to make a great writer. Make a list of criteria which can later help you to choose the winner. Also choose a jury spokesperson who will officiate at the contest.

STEP 4 – Hold the contest
The jury spokesperson welcomes everyone to the contest and invites the author groups to present and champion the authors in turn. The jury members listen carefully, taking notes, and then retire to discuss their impressions and opinions of the writers and to choose a winner. After they have made their decision, the jury spokesperson announces the result, sums up the reasons for the choice, and brings the contest to an end.

> **FACT FILE**
> The Man Booker Prize for Fiction is arguably the world's most important literary prize. Established in 1969, it is awarded annually to the best novel of the year written in English by a citizen of the Commonwealth or the Republic of Ireland. Not only does the winner receive £50,000, but because of the wide media coverage, every author on the final shortlist can always almost be sure of massive books sales worldwide.

The Man Booker Prize award ceremony in 2008

How to present a literary analysis

1. Set the context by introducing the author and then the book from which you have taken the passage or passages you are going to analyse.

2. Read the passages aloud, having first handed out copies so that everyone can follow more easily. Bear in mind that short extracts provide a concentrated focal point for listeners and are therefore usually more effective than long ones.

3. Analyse the passages you have read, picking out and commenting on features you think typify the author's skill e.g. descriptive powers, characterisation, dialogue, …

4. Conclude by summarising and reminding your listeners of the main strengths of the author. Finish on a high note that will create a lasting impression in their minds.

Project 2

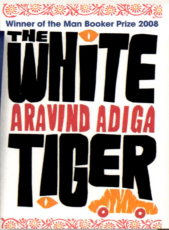

Talking about writers and novels: 10 strategies with useful phrases

Introducing a writer	Commenting on stylistic devices
I would like to tell you something about … He/She was born/grew up/now lives in … He/She started writing when … and has published … His/Her work is (greatly) influenced by … In addition to writing, …	The narrative perspective allows the reader to … The imagery evokes an atmosphere of … Foreshadowing has the effect of … The prose style/… reflects … The setting/… can be seen as an allegory of …
Outlining a novel	**Giving examples**
This is a work that combines the subgenres … It tells the story/explores the fate of … The events described take place/are set in … Among the main themes are …	For instance, look at … A good example of this is … Let me demonstrate this point by reading you … To illustrate what I mean, …
Explaining the narrative framework	**Describing the effect on the reader**
The novel is written in the form of … The story is narrated by … The reader follows events through the eyes of … The story moves backwards and forwards in time.	The reader is drawn into another world. It makes you want to read it again and again. An insight is given into … It is truly moving/mesmerising/…
Talking about the characters	**Giving praise**
The main/central protagonist is … He/She is characterised as … His/Her character is revealed/conveyed by … He/She goes through a … development: At first, …, but when … there is a massive change … His/Her function in the story is to … The relationship is important because …	There is no better novelist than … He/She is undoubtedly one of the finest writers ever. He/She is an author of exceptional talent/brilliance. His/Her novel is a true masterpiece. His/Her descriptions are wonderfully observed.
Describing the style of language	**Comparing writers**
The language is rich/poetic/vivid/imaginative/… There is frequent use of imagery/humour/… The descriptions are detailed/precise/… This author's style is innovative/individual/… The sentence structure is simple/complex/…	It is hard to make a direct comparison because … While he impresses by …, she … Compared to other writers, he … They are similar/different in that they … Of all the authors, …

Project 3

PROJECT 3: Myths and legends

First form two teams by choosing which part of the project you want to work on.
- In Part A you will compare the great ancient Indian epic the *Ramayana* with the European epic the *Iliad*.
- In Part B you will compare Bollywood with Hollywood.

At the end of the project each team will share their findings with the other team both by producing a written paper and by giving a class presentation.

A ANCIENT MYTHS: The Ramayana and the Iliad

STEP 1 – Organise and research
a) The team divides into two main groups to do separate research on the two epics. In order to make a comparison, you will need to research similar aspects of each, such as: date and origin; form and style; story and main themes; characters and archetypes; influence as a source of present-day cultural inspiration.
b) Each group develops a mind map to summarise and organise the information they have collected about their epic. The mind map should be poster-sized so that it is suitable for viewing as a group.

STEP 2 – Compare and prepare
a) The whole team comes back together to compare the group research results for the Ramayana and the Iliad. Use the mind maps you created in Step 1 to identify similarities and differences, and mark these in different colours so that they stand out visually.
b) Divide the team again into two new groups: one to produce the written paper and one to prepare an oral presentation supported by (audio)visual material. Both groups can use the marked mind maps to help structure their work. The initial focus should be on the Ramayana, with the Iliad then brought in as a comparison.

STEP 3 – Produce and present
Give your presentation and hand out copies of your paper for further reading.

How to plan and write an expository paper

- First research the information you need about your topic. At this stage there is no need for special organisation, but mind maps or notes can help to give a good overview of content.
- Now you have to decide how to order your material. There is no single correct way to do this as different topics and tasks require different treatment. Your approach should show a logical train of thought, however, and you should also always follow the general principles of developing a paper with a clear introduction, main part and conclusion.

- **Introduction:** State the overall topic and aim of the paper.
- **Main part:** Present and analyse the subject that is your main or initial focus. Then bring in any other specified subjects e.g. for comparison.
- **Conclusion:** Summarise the findings of your research.

- Make an outline showing the structure you want to follow and the focus of different paragraphs. Then write the paper in a clear, factual style.

Project 3

B MODERN LEGENDS: Bollywood and Hollywood

STEP 1 – Organise and research
a) The team divides into two main groups to do separate research on either Bollywood or Hollywood. Each main group then divides again into these two subgroups:
  1. **Background group:** Your task is to research the history of your film industry, the influences on it, and also its economic and cultural importance.
  2. **Analysis group:** Your task is to choose a film that is representative of your film industry, and then to select and analyse one or more scenes illustrating typical characteristics. In order to allow for a good comparison, the Hollywood group should look for a musical or love story.
b) Each subgroup should find a way to record their findings so that they can be easily shared with the rest of the team later, e.g. mind map, bullet points, grid.

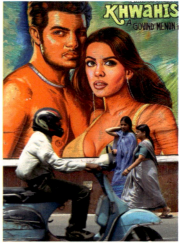

STEP 2 – Compare and prepare
a) The background subgroups from the two main groups meet to report and share their information. Together, they plan a written paper about Bollywood and how it compares with the Hollywood film industry.
b) The analysis subgroups from the two main groups meet to inform each other of their film choice and to compare the characteristic features of Bollywood and Hollywood productions. Together, they plan a presentation which will highlight any similarities or differences.
c) There is a final planning session when the whole team comes together to get an update and an overview of all the work. After listening to any comments or suggestions, the background groups write their paper and the analysis groups finalise the preparations for their presentation.

STEP 3 – Produce and present
Present your films to the class, starting with a suitable introduction and then going on to analyse and comment on your chosen scenes. At the end of the presentation hand out copies of the written paper for further reading.

How to present an archetypal film

- Start by giving some basic information about the film: genre, title, date, director, actors, production background etc.
- Briefly introduce the setting and context of each scene you show. In order to represent a particular film genre or production the scene should typify aspects such as plot, setting, characters, dialogue, body language, atmosphere.
- Also consider audiovisual aspects. Examine the use of cinematic devices like field size and camera angle and position, camera movement, editing technique, sound and music.

Field size and camera angle/position: The camera takes a long/medium/close-up/extreme close-up shot. • The camera position is … • The view on … is frontal/from above/below/behind. • The focus is on …

Camera movement: The camera zooms in/out of … • The camera pans/tilts from … to … • … is introduced in a panning/tilting shot. • The movement of … is followed in a tracking shot.

Editing: cut • fade in/out • The shots follow each other quickly./The shot stays on … for a while. • … is shown in slow/fast motion.

PROJECT 4: A taste of India

The standard greeting 'Have you eaten?' underlines the importance of food and hospitality in India. Indians believe it is an honour to share a meal with guests, and even the poorest of people are eager to offer what little they have to eat. This project culminates in a 'Taste of India' display which will enable you to learn and experience something of the vast range of traditions and flavours of a cuisine that is as diverse as the country itself.

STEP 1 – Choose your task
A: (3–4 students) Explore the historical, ethnic and religious influences which have resulted in the great variety and regional differences in Indian food.
B: (4–5 students) Research the historical importance of the spice trade, and collect information on the cultural, medicinal and culinary role of individual spices. Also create a typical Indian 'spice box' for your classmates to smell and taste. (As a starting point for this task, read 'The Mistress of Spices' on page 48/49!)
C: (1–2 students) Find out what elements constitute a traditional Indian meal and how certain kinds of dishes are combined to create a balanced diet.
D: (1–2 students) Research table manners and etiquette to establish how food is typically served and eaten in India.
E: (Rest of students) You are the cooks! Find recipes for a selection of dishes or snacks that can be eaten cold, e.g. chutneys, pickles, relishes, and different kinds of bread (chapati, parantha, naan etc.) to accompany them. Then prepare this food at home and bring it to school on the day of the display for everyone to sample.

STEP 2 – Make your contribution
Where you judge it to be necessary, share out and co-ordinate the work within your group. Then use suitable sources (the Internet, cookery books, personal connections etc.) to complete the task for which you are responsible. Study the ideas on the opposite page about how to create a varied display and consult with other groups to ensure that you use as many different forms of presentation as possible.

STEP 3 – Create your display
Set up the classroom as an exhibition arena for all your work and feast your senses on what you can see, smell and taste!

Project 4

How to create a successful display

- Organise your display so that each part of it deals with a different part of the overall theme. Put up large signs showing the focus of that particular section. Also consider whether you want to encourage people to view the display in a certain order or not.
- Achieve variety and stimulate interest by using as many different kinds of material as possible, e.g. labelled exhibits or samples to touch, smell, taste; fact sheets or handouts summarising information in bullet points, a grid or a mind map; posters with photos and captions; maps, diagrams etc.
- Combine different forms of presentation to complement each other. For example, a map could provide geographical reference points for information in a timeline, or recipe handouts could be offered next to food samples.
- Think practically about space, size etc. Can enough people view the same part of the display at the same time? Is the wording on a poster large enough to read from a reasonable distance? If people are allowed to touch or sample things, how are you going to keep that section tidy?

Sweet Lassi
Lassi is a drink that originated in Punjab and can have savoury or sweet flavourings.
Ingredients: 1 cup yogurt, 1 cup cold water, sugar to taste, 1 tsp rose water, pinch cardamom powder
Method: Blend together all the ingredients until frothy. Garnish with fresh mint leaves and serve as a cool, healthy and refreshing drink.

Useful vocabulary: Food preparation

Methods of cooking	Quantities and measurements	Flavours
Under a grill: **grilling** *On the hob:* **boiling** in a pan; **frying** in a frying pan; **stir-frying** in a wok; **deep-frying** in a fryer; **steaming** in a steamer; **pressure-cooking** *In the oven:* **roasting** in a roasting tin; **baking** on a baking-sheet or in a tin; **stewing** in a pot/casserole	ounce (oz) = 28.35 grams pound (lb) = 0.45 kilograms fluid ounce (fl.oz) = 0.028 litres pint (pt) = 0.570 litres table/dessert/teaspoon level/heaped spoonful a pinch … … to taste	sweet/sugary savoury sour bitter mild spicy hot/peppery salty

Kitchen utensils and their use

chopping board to prepare food on
sharp knife for cutting, chopping and slicing
peeler for peeling vegetables and fruit
grater for grating cheese, vegetables etc.
rolling pin for rolling out pastry or dough
mortar and pestle for grinding herbs and spices
sieve for sifting flour
colander for draining off water
wooden spoon for beating or stirring mixtures
tongs for picking up or turning hot food
whisk for whisking or whipping eggs or liquids
food processor for mixing, blending, liquidising etc.

Worksheets

VOCABULARY WORK

Learning vocabulary is essential to language learning: The more words and collocations or connections between words you know, the better you will be able to communicate your ideas and succeed in your exams. It is never too early to start learning vocabulary systematically!

This is where our vocabulary concept can help you. You can learn and revise vocabulary by working with the vocabulary files on the accompanying CD. Find out which way of working with the vocabulary files suits you best and try to apply the new words you learn wherever possible.

The vocabulary files on the CD
The CD contains two types of vocabulary files: Text-based vocabulary files, which are closely linked with the texts in this book, and thematic vocabulary files, which list the most important words and phrases connected with the seven topical fields dealt with in this book.

All the vocabulary files are made up of three columns:
1. The left-hand column is for the word or phrase to be learned.
   (Notes on pronunciation or stress can be added where necessary.)
2. The right-hand column is for the German translation.
3. The middle column is for anything that helps you remember the word or phrase and how to use it, e. g.

- words from the same word family
- paraphrases, synonyms, antonyms, false friends
- example sentences and collocations
- pictures or drawings

All vocabulary files can be edited with a word processor on a computer, so you can easily add new words and phrases that are presented in class.

Symbols and abbreviations

adj	adjective	*infml*	informal
adv	adverb	*n*	noun, substantive
AE	American English	*pej*	pejorative
↔	antonym	*sb*	somebody
BE	British English	*sl*	slang
coll	collocation	*sth*	something
disappr	disapproving	*syn*	synonym
esp	especially	*v*	verb
≠	false friends	*vlg*	vulgar
fml	formal	→	from the same word family
hum	humorous		

Vocabulary wo...

How to work with the text-based vocabulary files

These vocabulary files contain the most important words and phrases from the book. They are listed in the order in which they occur in the texts. There is one vocabulary file for each text in the book. As you will see, they are not complete. Filling in what is missing is part of the learning process.

What you can do with them:
- Use the relevant text and a dictionary to complete the files.
- Add more information or vocabulary individually.
- Use a computer or print them out and fill them in by hand.
- Use them as worksheets for homework and exam preparation.
- Reduce, rearrange or add to the lists and turn them into vocabulary tests or quizzes for a partner, or you may have other ideas of your own. It's up to you!

Text-based vocabulary file

Topic 1 – A plural country		Indian identity is forged from diversity, p. 6/7
Word/phrase	**Usage/memory aid**	**Translation**
to require	• What qualifications are required for this position? • → requirement (n)	etw. erfordern, brauchen
inconceivable	It is inconceivable that Tom would leave his family. They are everything to him.	unvorstellbar, undenkbar
startling	• These are startling results. • surprising/amazing/astonishing	überraschend, verblüffend

How to work with the thematic vocabulary files

These vocabulary files contain the most important words and phrases for discussing the main themes in the book. The topics include:
A History and politics, B Life in India, C Behaviour and feelings.
The vocabulary words are given in alphabetical order. You needn't complete these files, but they can also be edited and worked with in the same way as the text-based files. They are especially useful for your exam preparation.

Thematic vocabulary file

History and politics		
Word/phrase	**Usage/memory aid**	**Translation**
to abandon	to abandon a way of life/an idea/ship/a child	aufgeben; aussetzen
act	a law passed by the government	Gesetz
administration	The town council is a board of local administration.	Verwaltung
to aid	to help, to support, to give assistance	helfen; unterstützen
to allocate	▪ → allocation (n) ▪ The Red Cross have to allocate food to the whole country after the flood.	bereitstellen, zuteilen

59

REVISION FILE 1: A plural country (Topic 1)

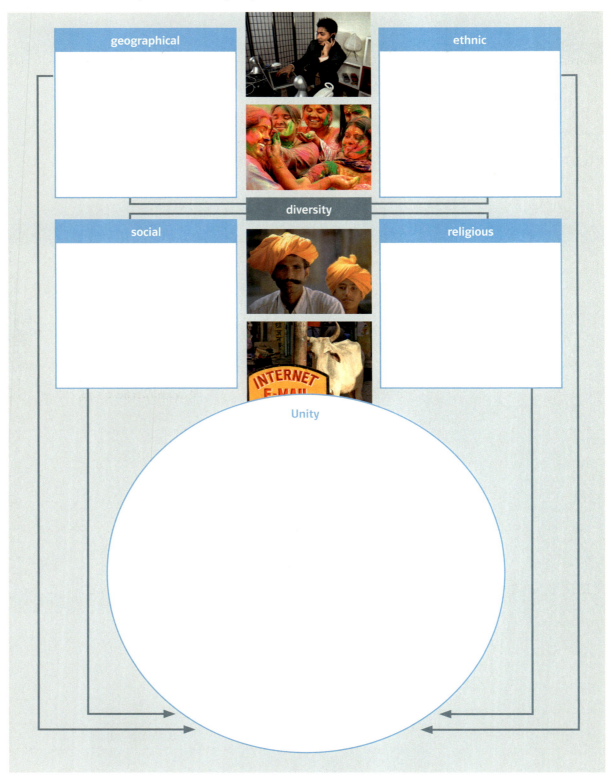

Revision file 2

REVISION FILE 2: **The wounds of history** (Topic 2)

Describe the social and political problems India faces today.

Muslims in India	Pakistan	International relations

Now try to link the present situaion with historical events / developments. The following keywords might help you:
partition • Jinnah • Gandhi • viceroy • World War II • …

Show/Visualise the relations between the different events by drawing arrows.

REVISION FILE 3: Different worlds (Topic 3)

Collect key information about different groups in India and fill the appropriate boxes. Then think about the implications for the future.

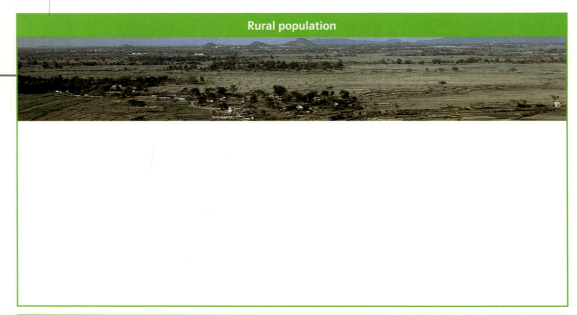

Rural population

Urban population

Hopes and challenges for the future:

Revision file 4

REVISION FILE 4: East meets West (Topic 4)

*In (the texts of) this chapter you have learnt that East and West interact in different ways.
Name facts from the texts that show Eastern influence on the West and the other way round.*

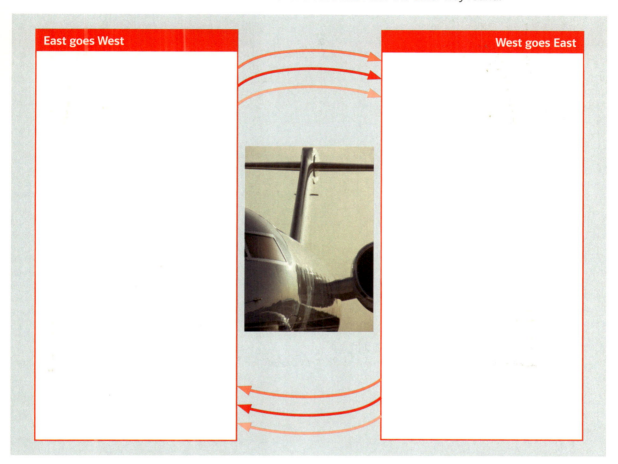

East goes West

West goes East

What role does Eastern influence play in your life?

Eastern influence in my life

Acknowledgements

Text and song credits: 6–7 © Guardian News & Media Ltd 2007; **8–9** Used by permission of A P Watt Ltd, London, on behalf of Edward Luce; **11** From *Point No Point* by Sujata Bhatt © Carcanet Press Limited, 1997; **12–13** Reprinted by permission of HarperCollins Publishers Ltd © William Dalrymple 1998; **15** From *A Passage to India* by E. M. Forster © The Provost and Scholars of King's College, Cambridge; **16–17** © Guardian News & Media Ltd 2007; **18** Reprinted by permission of SLL/Sterling Lord Literistic, Inc. Copyright by Bapsi Sidhwa; **20–21** © 2007 Pankaj Mishra; **22–23** © 2008 *Los Angeles Times*; **24** Used by permission of A P Watt Ltd, London, on behalf of Edward Luce; **25** © SPIEGEL ONLINE, 5. Dezember 2008; **28–29** © 2002 *Asian News*, www.theasiannews.co.uk/ This article first appeared in The Guardian; **30–31** From *Nectar in a Sieve* by Kamala Markandaya © HarperCollins Publishers, New York; **32–33** By David Davidar, *The Solitude of Emperors*, Weidenfeld and Nicolson, an imprint of The Orion Publishing Group; **34–35** © 2007 Channel 4, www.channel4.com; **36–37** © South Asian Women's Forum, 2005, www.sawf.org; **38–39** From *The God of Small Things* by Arundhati Roy, used by permission of David Godwin Associates; **40–41** Excerpted from "The World as India" from *At the same time* by Susan Sontag Copyright © The Estate of Susan Sontag 2007. Reproduced by permission. All rights reserved.; **42–43** Copyright © Cape Cod Scriveners Co., 2007; **44** © 2006 *The Sunday Times*; **45** © 2006 Christiane Grefe, DIE ZEIT, N° 39/2006; **46–47** From *Jasmine* by Bharati Mukherjee © HarperCollins Publishers, New York; **48–49** From *The Mistress of Spices* by Chitra Banerjee Divakaruni © Random House Group Limited, London, 1998; **51** © Trailfinders Worldwide 2009, www.trailfinders.com

Picture credits: U1.1 Corbis (Peter Adams), Düsseldorf; **U1.2** shutterstock, New York, NY; **U1.3** shutterstock, New York, NY; **U1.4** laif (Bernd Jonkmanns), Köln; **U1.5** shutterstock, New York, NY; **U1.6** JupiterImages photos.com, Tucson, AZ; **1.1** Avenue Images GmbH (Image Source), Hamburg; **4.1** Guardian News & Media Ltd 2007; **4.2+3** Wright's Reprints, Texas; **5.1** Christian Dekelver, Weinstadt; **6.1** shutterstock (Jeremy Richards), New York, NY; **7.1** Alamy Images (Eric Nathan), Abingdon, Oxon; **8.1** shutterstock (ARTEKI), New York, NY; **8.2** shutterstock (Jeremy Richards), New York, NY; **8.3** shutterstock (Mark Rhiggins), New York, NY; **9.1** Fotolia LLC (Melissa Schalke), New York; **10.1** Corbis (Bettmann), Düsseldorf; **11.1** shutterstock (Vishal Shah), New York, NY; **11.2** shutterstock (Sverlova Mariya), New York, NY; **11.3** Carcanet Press, Manchester; **12.1** Fotolia LLC (TMAX), New York; **13.1** shutterstock (Luciano Mortula), New York, NY; **14.1** Picture-Alliance (imagestate/HI), Frankfurt; **14.2** Ullstein Bild GmbH (TopFoto), Berlin; **15.1** Corbis (Hulton-Deutsch Collection), Düsseldorf; **16.1** Interfoto, München; **17.1** The Associated Press GmbH (Anil Kapoor Films Company), Frankfurt am Main; **18.1** Milkweed Editions, Minneapolis; **19.1** Alamy Images (Sebastian Wasek), Abingdon, Oxon; **19.2** Getty Images (NARINDER NANU/AFP), München; **20.1** laif (Keystone France/Eyedea Presse), Köln; **20.2+3** Corbis (Bettmann), Düsseldorf; **21.1** Corbis, Düsseldorf; **22.1** Corbis (Ramin Talaie), Düsseldorf; **22.2** The Associated Press GmbH (Lefteris Pitarakis), Frankfurt am Main; **23.1** Getty Images (AAMIR QURESHI/AFP), München; **24.1** Getty Images (Chris Hondros), München; **26.1** laif (REA), Köln; **26.2** Fotolia LLC (GAMUT STOCK IMAGES), New York; **26.3** shutterstock (Vishal Shah), New York, NY; **26.4** Alamy Images (David R. Frazier Photolibrary, Inc.), Abingdon, Oxon; **26.5** shutterstock (Vishal Shah), New York, NY; **27.1** shutterstock (Regien Paassen), New York, NY; **27.2** laif (Bernd Jonkmanns), Köln; **27.3** Ullstein Bild GmbH (Reuters), Berlin; **27.4** Fotolia LLC (Ronnie), New York; **27.5** shutterstock (Girish Menon), New York, NY; **28.1** Corbis (Frédéric Soltan), Düsseldorf; **29.1** shutterstock (Vladimir Melnik), New York, NY; **30.1** Fotosearch Stock Photography (Digital Vision), Waukesha, WI; **31.1** Unionsverlag, Zürich; **32.1** Corbis, Düsseldorf; **32.2** Corbis (Neil Emmerson/Robert Harding World Imagery), Düsseldorf; **33.1** David Davidar, The Solitude of Emperors, Weidenveld and Nicolson, an imprint of the Orion Publ. Group; **33.2** Mauritius Images (Erik Bohr), Mittenwald; **34.1+2** Corbis (Jon Hicks), Düsseldorf; **35.1** AKG (Rainer Hackenberg), Berlin; **36.1** Alamy Images (Wayne Tippetts), Abingdon, Oxon; **36.2** Corbis, Düsseldorf; **36.3** laif (Bernd Jonkmanns), Köln; **36.4** shutterstock (Phil Date), New York, NY; **36.5** Fotolia LLC (Günter Menzl), New York; **37.1** laif, Köln; **37.2** www.cartoonstock.com (Kes), Bath; **37.3** Interfoto (NG Collection), München; **39.1** Ullstein Bild GmbH (Vario-Press), Berlin; **40.1** iStockphoto (Alexander S. Heitkamp), Calgary, Alberta; **40.2** laif (Evelyn Hockstein/The New York Times/Redux), Köln; **40.3** Corbis, Düsseldorf; **40.4** Getty Images (Polly Borland), München; **41.1** www.cartoonstock.com (Fran), Bath; **42.1** iStockphoto (kshishtof), Calgary, Alberta; **42.2** shutterstock (Vera Bogaerts), New York, NY; **42.3** laif (Monier Louis/Gamma/Eyedea Presse), Köln; **43.1** iStockphoto (Nitin Sanil), Calgary, Alberta; **43.2** shutterstock (salamanderman), New York, NY; **44.1** FOCUS (Adrian Fisk), Hamburg; **44.2** Imago Stock & People, Berlin; **45.1** Cinetext GmbH (Kinowelt), Frankfurt; **46.1** Corbis (Lee Snider/Photo Images), Düsseldorf; **47.1** The Associated Press GmbH (Marty Lederhandler), Frankfurt am Main; **48.1** Corbis (Lew Robertson), Düsseldorf; **49.1** Wikimedia Foundation Inc. (PD), St. Petersburg FL; **50.1** Geoatlas, Hendaye; **50.2** Alamy Images (Peter Titmuss), Abingdon, Oxon; **51.1** Fotolia LLC (Syphoto), New York; **52.1** Getty Images (Eamonn McCormack), München; **53.1** Penguin Group (UK), London WC2R ORL; **53.2** The Random House Group Limited, London; **53.3** Atlantic Books, London; **53.4** HarperCollins, London-Hammersmith; **54.1** shutterstock (Juha Sompinmäki), New York, NY; **54.2** AKG, Berlin; **55.1** Picture-Alliance, Frankfurt; **55.2** Cinetext GmbH (rem), Frankfurt; **56.1** shutterstock, New York, NY; **56.2** Imago Stock & People, Berlin; **57.1** shutterstock (Monkey Business Images), New York, NY; **57.2** Getty Images (punchstock), München; **58.1** Bananastock, Watlington/Oxon; **60.1** shutterstock (Peter Albrektsen), New York, NY; **60.2** Picture-Alliance (dap/epa/Manjunath Kiran), Frankfurt; **60.3** MEV Verlag GmbH, Augsburg; **60.4** shutterstock (Vladimir Melnik), New York, NY; **62.1** Nissel, Wien; **62.2** shutterstock (salamanderman), New York, NY; **63.1** Getty Images RF (Photo Disc), München

Every effort has been made to locate owners of copyright material, but in a few cases this has not proved possible and repeated inquiries have remained unanswered. The publishers would be glad to hear from any further copyright owners of material reproduced in this book.